Hampshire and Dorset

Car Tours

Anne-Marie Edwards

Acknowledgements

I would like to thank the staff of all the Tourist Information Centres in Hampshire and Dorset for their unfailing friendly help and advice, particularly Mrs Judith Burrows in Blandford Forum. As always, my research has been a pleasure owing to the help I receive from the staff at Southampton and Totton libraries. I am grateful to Heather Pearson, Sandy Sims and other members of the publishing team at the Ordnance Survey for checking the routes. Finally, I thank my husband Mike who accompanied me.

Front cover photograph: *Okeford Fitzpaine, Dorset*
Title page photograph: *Wherwell, Hampshire*

Author and Series Editor: Anne-Marie Edwards
Editor: Paula Granados, Donald Greig
Designers: Brian Skinner, Ellen Moorcraft
Photographs: Jarrold Publishing, except for p16: Hampshire County
    Museum Service

Ordnance Survey   ISBN 0-3190-0621-2
Jarrold Publishing   ISBN 0-7117-0845-2

First published 1996 by Ordnance Survey and Jarrold Publishing

Ordnance Survey   Jarrold Publishing
Romsey Road   Whitefriars
Maybush   Norwich NR3 1TR
Southampton SO16 4GU

Printed in Great Britain by Jarrold Book Printing, Thetford, Norfolk 1/96

CONTENTS

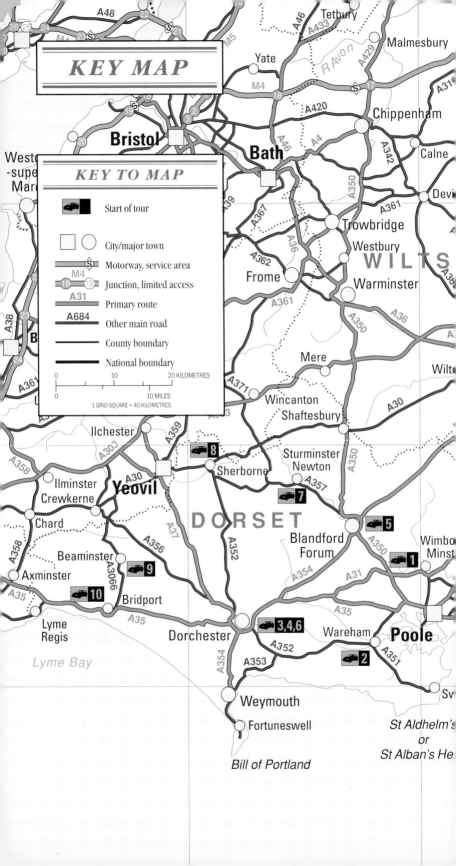

KEY MAP

KEY TO MAP

🚗⬛ Start of tour

⬜ ⬭ City/major town

━Ⓢ━ Motorway, service area

⟨18⟩━⟨19⟩ Junction, limited access

A31 Primary route

A684 Other main road

──── County boundary

──── National boundary

0 ———— 10 ———— 20 KILOMETRES
0 ———— 10 MILES
1 GRID SQUARE = 40 KILOMETRES

Tetbury

Malmesbury

Yate

Chippenham

Bristol

Bath

Calne

Devi

Westo-super-Mare

Trowbridge

Westbury

W I L T S

Frome

Warminster

Mere

Wilt

Ilchester

Wincanton

Shaftesbury

🚗 8

Sturminster Newton

Ilminster

Crewkerne

Yeovil

Sherborne

🚗 7

D O R S E T

🚗 5

Chard

Blandford Forum

Wimbo Minst

Beaminster

Axminster

🚗 9

🚗 1

🚗 10

Bridport

🚗 3,4,6

Wareham

Poole

Lyme Regis

Dorchester

🚗 2

Lyme Bay

Weymouth

Sv

Fortuneswell

St Aldhelm's or St Alban's He

Bill of Portland

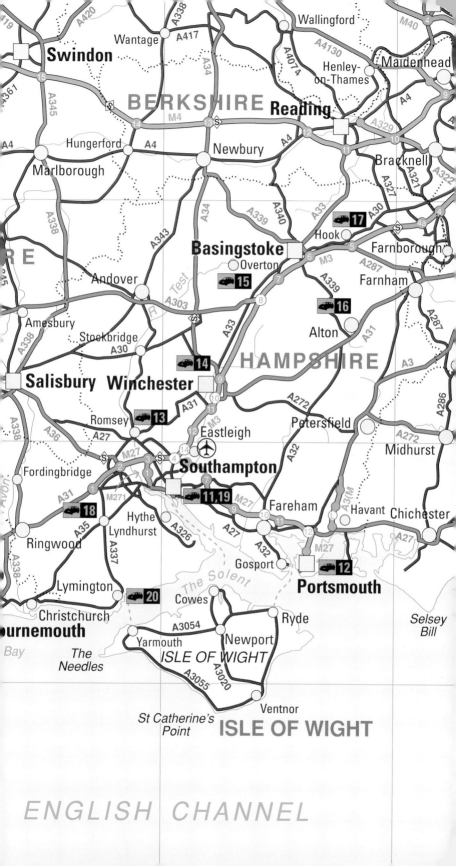

INTRODUCTION
TO HAMPSHIRE

At first glance it may seem that this southern county fringing the Solent shore lacks the dramatic scenery of the more obvious touring areas such as the West Country or the Lake District. But within its 1,457 square miles is some of the loveliest and most interesting country in England. Not spectacular, true, but countryside that in all respects is typically English. Here are wide downland vistas, steep wooded hills, lush river valleys threaded by fine trout and salmon rivers, and old-world villages of cob, flint and thatch. Add to these a coastline that has witnessed the greatest events in England's history. Hampshire also possesses a unique treasure, the New Forest. Created for the royal hunt by William the Conqueror in 1079, over 120 square miles of rolling heaths and magnificent ancient woodlands still remain in the south-west corner of Hampshire, open for all to explore.

Man has settled in this comfortable county from earliest times, leaving a rich legacy of historical sites. Only a few of Hampshire's towns have outgrown their attractiveness, most are small market towns with mainly Georgian houses lining their wide high streets. Set like a jewel in the heart of the county is Winchester, renowned for its magnificent cathedral. But even the humblest village will reward the visitor. Tiny Corhampton, tucked away in the Meon valley, is graced by one of the most perfectly preserved of all Saxon churches.

A unique breed of ponies with a wild ancestry roams freely in the New Forest

Hampshire is a county of contrasts. To appreciate this, imagine that you are standing on the crest of Portsdown Hill, the great chalk ridge dominating Portsmouth Harbour. Looking south, Portsmouth lies at your feet, spreading over Portsea Island. It has been the home of the Royal Navy since Henry VII established the earliest known dry dock near the site of No. 2 Dock, where HMS *Victory* now rests, to service his small fleet of warships. But, hundreds of years earlier, Portsmouth Harbour had been valued as a convenient base for assembling a fleet for trade and military purposes. The Romans established a fort at Portchester at the head of the harbour, and in the twelfth century a small town developed around the

Winchester Cathedral. Building began in 1079 under Bishop Walklyn and the earliest church was consecrated in 1093.

Camber, a natural inlet. This was fortified by Edward III during the Hundred Years' War, and remained the heart of Portsmouth's military garrison. Beyond the narrow harbour entrance lies the Solent with the deep channel where, for centuries, British warships have anchored off Spithead. Across the water rise the downs of the Isle of Wight. East of the harbour is tranquil Langstone Harbour, its shallow waters green with eel-grass, a sanctuary for wildlife.

West of your vantage point on Portsdown Hill is the River Hamble, world famous as a yachting centre. Yet, within a stone's throw of this busy scene are quiet nature reserves. Further west, Southampton lies at the head of Southampton Water at the confluence of the rivers Test and Itchen. Benefiting from a deep and easy approach, double high tides and convenient access to the continent, the town developed in the nineteenth century into England's foremost passenger port, when it became the headquarters of the Royal Mail, Union Castle and Cunard steamship lines. Today, great liners still make use of its fine docks, and Southampton is a leading container port. But it is also a historic city with part of its medieval walls and many interesting old buildings. Beyond the industrial complex fronting Southampton Water is the unchanged landscape of the New Forest and the bird-haunted marshes around Lymington.

Turn northwards from Portsdown Hill and the view is entirely different. It is one of almost continuous undulating countryside.

A satisfying blend of cornfields, leafy hedgerows and small woods
cover the lower chalk hills which gradually rise to the superb
uplands around the Bourne valley in the north-west, and the more
dramatic escarpments around Selborne in the east. The rivers Test,
Itchen and Meon rise in the uplands and flow gently southwards
through folds in the downs, carving wide valleys. Here are villages
untouched by time. Itchen Abbas, where Charles Kingsley wrote most
of *The Water Babies*; Wherwell, clustered around the remains of an
abbey founded by the Saxon queen Elfrida; and East Meon, with its
fifteenth-century court-house and Norman church, are just three
of Hampshire's treasures waiting to be discovered.

Only a few miles to the north of Portsdown the chalk uplands
reach their highest southerly point, 889 feet (271 metres), at Butser
Hill. This is an ancient landscape dotted with prehistoric burial
mounds and scored with Iron Age ramparts and ditches. An Iron
Age settlement has been reconstructed close by and forms part of
the Queen Elizabeth Country Park, one of many delightful family-
orientated parks to be found throughout the county. Three miles
north of Butser is the charming market town of Petersfield, sheltered
by downs which inspired the poetry of Edward Thomas. Further
east, the chalk descends abruptly to greensand rocks creating beech-
covered 'hangers'. This is the country of Gilbert White whose famous
book *The Natural History of Selborne* has run into many editions
since its publication in 1788. The gentler farming countryside to
the north, with its scattering of small villages and manors, formed
the inspiration and setting for the novels of one of England's greatest
novelists, Jane Austen. At Steventon near Basingstoke (then a small
market town) and later at Chawton Cottage near Alton, she found
the settled country life that enabled her to write. Tour 15 is a special
'Jane Austen' tour.

Hambledon village where the rules of English cricket were devised

Within such a diverse area as Hampshire it is not surprising to find a great wealth of stately homes, most of them open for visitors. Outstanding among them must be Palace House at Beaulieu in the New Forest; Stratfield Saye, the gift of a grateful Nation to the Duke of Wellington; Broadlands, once the home of Lord Palmerston and, more recently, Earl Mountbatten of Burma; and The Vyne, which possesses the best late-medieval private chapel in England. Many beautiful gardens include special delights, such as the National Trust's collection of old-fashioned roses at Mottisfont and the recreated sixteenth-century garden at the Tudor House in Southampton.

Hampshire has moved with the times, but has not forgotten its rich heritage. Today, owing to the work of the County Council, the National Trust, and other responsible bodies, that heritage is ours to enjoy.

Picturesque cottages at Lower Froyle

INTRODUCTION TO DORSET

Dorset is rural England at its most tranquil and unhurried. There are no large towns, little industry and few major roads. Thomas Hardy would still recognise the peaceful villages and small market towns he immortalised in his novels. Some changes have taken place of course – much of the wild gorse-covered moorland Hardy named 'Egdon Heath' has been planted with pines – but Dorset retains its essential character and its power to charm.

Part of Dorset's attraction must lie in the wide variety of its scenery owing to the ever-changing nature of the underlying rock. It is said that after a tour of Dorset you will have seen three-quarters of England! The breath-taking beauty of the Dorset coast running east from Lyme Regis to Christchurch on the Hampshire border is justly famous. From Lyme Regis a wonderful line of cliffs stretches for over 20 miles to Portland Bill. Alternate layers of greensand, limestone rock and clay produce cliff faces of many colours which rise to their highest point at Golden Cap. Through them small streams and rivers carve delightful combes. The sheer sandstone cliffs framing West Bay at the mouth of the River Brit are protected by the beginning of Chesil Beach, a great bank of pebbles smoothed and shaped by the sea running for 18 miles to Portland and trapping behind it the sheltered waters of the Fleet. These waters have been a haven for swans for over six hundred years, and the swannery at Abbotsbury is a 'must' for all visitors to Dorset. Portland is a world apart, reaching out from the coast like the beak of a bird, shielding the sands of Weymouth

The Dorset coast near Charmouth, rich in fossils

10

The 'planned' village of Milton Abbas designed by 'Capability' Brown in 1768 for the Earl of Dorchester

from the force of south-westerly gales. More magnificent cliffs march eastwards to meet the great barrier of chalk hills that crosses the Isle of Purbeck. Spectacular white cliffs rise sheer from the sea with isolated rocks, like the well-known 'Old Harry', separated from the mainland and washed on all sides by the waves. Swanage and Studland Bay are tucked cosily within headlands. Nature reserves lead to the old town of Wareham at the mouth of the River Frome and form the western shores of Poole Harbour. From the old port of Poole boat trips can be made round the harbour's numerous inlets and islands. A highlight is a visit to Brownsea Island, a paradise for wildlife. Bournemouth offers sandy beaches and beautiful gardens and the ancient town of Christchurch its lovely, almost landlocked, harbour and splendid priory church.

Inland from the coastal downs the main Dorset rivers, the Cerne, the Frome, the Piddle, the Stour and the Allen, carve narrow valleys through chalk uplands before flowing through fertile flood plains into their common outlet, Poole Harbour. The county town, Dorchester, stands within the embankments of its Roman walls at the confluence of the rivers Cerne and Frome. A fascinating small town, it is still the important meeting place at the centre of Dorset life that Thomas Hardy pictured in his novels. The great novelist was born only a few miles away at Higher Bockhampton. Tour 3 visits his birthplace and the countryside most closely associated with him. The market for the beautiful Stour valley is Blandford Forum, an elegant Georgian town. Further south, where the River Stour is joined by the River Allen, lies Wimborne Minster,

its picturesque courts and alley-ways overlooked by the most homely and charming of churches.

North of these small towns is a country of high chalk hills which rise to almost 1,000 feet (305 metres) at Pilsdon Pen and around Bulbarrow. From the smooth turf of these windswept downs there are panoramic views south across the Purbeck range to the Isle of Wight and north to the Mendips. East of the River Stour is Cranborne Chase, formerly a royal hunting forest, and still the haunt of wild deer. Areas of unimproved downland rich in wild flowers, butterflies and birds are carefully preserved. Beyond the chalk hills Dorset springs its greatest surprise! Suddenly, the chalk escarpment ceases and leading away from its foot, as far as the eye can see, is the Blackmoor Vale, a green, undulating world of small fields and hedges, dotted with woods and scattered hamlets. It is wonderful touring country and still merits Frederick Treves' description written in 1906 in his book *Highways and Byways in Dorset*. He writes of the Vale as 'that valley of the Blue Mist in whose soft shadows will be found the very heart of England'. Dorset's fine poet, William Barnes, also captured the beauty of the Vale in his verse.

Throughout the county there are reminders of the past. Most of the downland summits are ringed with the embankments of Neolithic and Iron Age forts, and just

Wareham Quay. Today it is popular with pleasure craft, once it was the hub of a busy port.

south of Dorchester is the great fort of Maiden Castle, dating back to 3,700 BC. Ancient trackways follow the crests of the hills, and the 180-foot- (55 metres) long outline of the giant cut into the chalk above Cerne Abbas village still puzzles historians. Medieval farming methods have scored the hillsides with strip lynchets. Early Christianity was lovingly fostered in Sherborne and Wimborne Minster and in Dorset's many other abbeys. Memories of the Civil War linger in many Dorset villages and swords hidden after the Monmouth rebellion are still being found buried in the thatch.

And, perhaps, it is in the county's villages that Dorset's greatest charm lies. Their evocative names, such as Ryme Intrinseca, Fontmell Magna, Melbury Bubb, Okeford Fitzpaine, Sydling St Nicholas and Hammoon, hint at their special magic. Turn a corner and there stands an old manor built of creamy white or golden stone beside an unassuming church which may well date from Saxon times and be decorated with medieval wall paintings. Close by is a handful of low, darkly thatched cottages. The Dorset village makes no attempt to impress, but the effect of this timeless scene is truly enchanting.

ENJOY YOUR TOUR

The tours in this book have been designed to cover Hampshire and Dorset as comprehensively as possible. Towns have been chosen as starting points for ease of access, but as all the tours are circular they can be started from any point on the route. It is a good plan to read the tours through before starting. Both counties contain so much of interest that must be included in the route of the tour, often requiring visits of a half or even a whole day to do them justice, that it is best to see the tours as 'menus' and decide beforehand which attractions you prefer. The times given for each tour cover motoring only and, of course, can only be approximate. To make the tours easier to follow the navigational instructions have been printed in bold. There are also boxed letters which tie in with those on the map. Their purpose is to aid navigation and, in many instances, highlight sections of the route requiring particular attention. It is possible that opening times for the various attractions may have changed and it is advisable to telephone before visiting. For planning walks in scenic areas you will find the Pathfinder guides, Pathfinder maps or the OS Outdoor Leisure maps at 1: 25 000 (2½ inches to 1 mile/4 cm to 1 km) are ideal. For details see inside back cover.

In order to see some of the loveliest areas it has been necessary to include limited stretches of narrow roads. Give way to impatient users who may have a train to catch! Be particularly careful on roads in the New Forest. Most minor roads in the area have speed limits. Ponies, deer, geese, donkeys and pigs are fully aware that their right-of-way on the roads was established in Saxon times, so watch out for them, especially at night! It is always dangerous to feed or pet the ponies as they are wild and unpredictable. If they insist on sharing your picnic, move on.

WIMBORNE MINSTER, CRANBORNE CHASE AND THE TARRANT VALLEY

49 MILES – 4 HOURS
START AND FINISH AT WIMBORNE MINSTER

This tour travels through some of the finest countryside in southern England. Gentle pastoral scenes beside the River Allen give way to the rolling grasslands dotted with the beech woods of Cranborne Chase. The return route follows the peaceful valley of the River Tarrant, weaving past a succession of old-world villages. Historical interest includes visits to Rockbourne Roman Villa and Badbury Rings, and there is an opportunity to visit one of the most magnificent seventeenth-century houses in Dorset, Kingston Lacy.

• PLACES OF INTEREST •

Wimborne Minster
Wimborne Minster is a pleasant market town set in green meadows threaded by two rivers, the Allen and the Stour.
Interesting old streets containing many fine Georgian buildings cluster around its splendid minster which is like no other church. The multi-coloured stonework of its twin towers convey a homely, friendly impression. On the north face of the west tower a wooden 'quarter Jack' in the brightly painted uniform of a grenadier from the Napoleonic wars strikes the quarter hours. Inside, Saxon foundations support heavy Norman arches and a magnificent central Norman tower. All other architectural periods are also represented here, up to the fifteenth century. The minster's many treasures include a Saxon chest, a remarkable fourteenth-century astronomical clock, the Beaufort tomb, and a glowing medieval glass window said to

have been made in Flanders. Above the vestry is the chained library founded in 1686 containing over 240 books, including a fourteenth-century manuscript on vellum. The library is open to the public Easter–October, Monday–Friday, 10–4.
In the High Street is the Priest's House set in beautiful gardens stretching down to the mill stream. This fine Elizabethan building houses the **Museum of East Dorset Life**, recreating 400 years of history through a series of period rooms from Jacobean to Victorian times. Open 1 April– 28 October, Monday–Saturday, 10.30–5. Also June–September, Sundays, 2–5. Telephone: Wimborne (01202) 882533
West of the minster is **Wimborne Minster Model Town and Gardens**. Visitor and Exhibition Centre. Refreshments, gift shop, plants for sale. Open 7 April–1 October, daily, 10–5. Telephone: (01202) 881924

Leave Wimborne Minster heading north along the B3078 signed Cranborne. The road crosses the River Allen and then runs along the valley on the right bank of the river to Stanbridge. About a mile further turn left signposted Witchampton **A** to cross the river. The bridge bears a plaque often seen in Dorset threatening any would-be vandal with transportation for life! As you enter Witchampton pass a lane on the left signposted The Tarrants. The road then bears left past

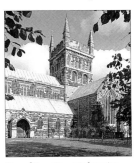

One of Dorset's most charming treasures – Wimborne Minster

Abbey House on the right and the church on the left. Abbey House, built of rose-coloured bricks, is said to be one of the oldest manors in Dorset. **Just past the church turn left signposted Manswood and Long Crichel. At the T-junction turn right. Keep ahead past a turning on the right and, in just over a mile, turn right signposted Moor Crichel.**

The road bears right round the northern limit of Moor Crichel park signposted **Gussage All Saints and then crosses a stream and runs to a T-junction. Turn right, signposted Horton, to bridge the River Allen and rejoin the B3078. Turn left signposted Horton and Cranborne. After about a mile turn left down a lane signposted Brockington.** On the right is a parking area beside the historic Knowlton Circles. The ruins of a tiny Norman church are encircled by high grass covered embankments.

The wooded slopes of Cranborne Chase

The Circles date from late neolithic times, around 2,500 BC.

Continue past Brockington Farm to a T-junction. Turn right to follow the road to Wimborne St Giles. In the village the road bears a little right signed for Cranborne. Park beside the green to explore Wimborne St Giles. Flint and brick cottages, many thatched, overlook wide lawns, and a row of seventeenth-century almshouses leads to a church lost among the trees. One of the

trees, a magnificent yew, is said to be two thousand years old! The village has grown up around St Giles House, built in 1650 by Anthony Ashley-Cooper, first Earl of Shaftesbury.

Continue through the village and turn right along the B3081 signposted Ringwood to meet the B3078. After about ½ mile turn left for Cranborne. Drive into the centre of the village and turn right following the signs to the car park. Once a bustling

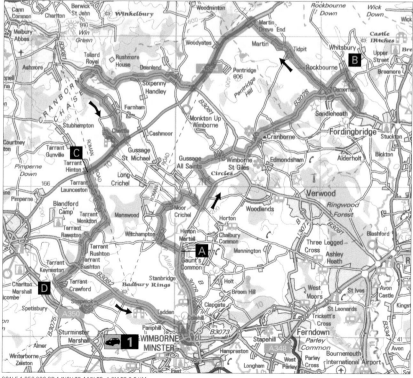

SCALE 1:250 000 OR 1 INCH TO 4 MILES *1 CM TO 2.5 KM*

15

One of the fine mosaic floors at Rockbourne Roman Villa

town, the capital of the hunting forest of Cranborne Chase, it is now an attractive village of pleasant red brick houses clustered around quiet streets merging into gardens. There is a good view of its mainly Jacobean manor from the public footpath beside the churchyard.

From Cranborne continue along the road signposted Damerham. The road runs through the beautiful beech woods of the Chase before bearing right at a Y-junction signposted Fordingbridge. In Damerham the road turns left and crosses the River Allen. The road turns right for Fordingbridge. In a little over a mile, just after the Sandleheath village sign, turn left signposted Rockbourne Roman Villa. The entrance to the car park for the villa and museum is signed off the road on the left. The villa has an idyllic setting surrounded by low wooded hillsides. The museum gives a lively picture of day-to-day life in Roman times.

The 100-foot- (30.5m) high monument on the hill commemorates Sir Eyre Coote who served with Clive in India. **The tour continues along the valley to Rockbourne village, beautifully sited on the banks of a clear chalk stream. Drive through the rows of thatched cottages and look carefully for a lane on the right leading off a left bend. Turn right up the lane and then turn right**

again following the sign for the church. There is a parking area on the left. Leave the car and follow the lane past Rockbourne Manor to climb to the church which has retained many Saxon features. From the churchyard you look down on the manor which is partly Elizabethan and has the remains of a thirteenth-century chapel. Footpaths lead past the church to Whitsbury Iron Age hill-fort.

Retrace the route through Rockbourne and take the first turning on the right signposted Damerham 🄱. At the T-junction turn right for Martin along the valley of the River Allen. The road crosses the line of Grim's Ditch, an ancient earthwork, and climbs through Martin, a long village of mainly thatched cottages almost hidden in a fold of the downs. W.H. Hudson, the author of *A Shepherd's Life*, based the character of Shepherd Bawcombe on a friend who lived in Martin.

Continue to meet the A354 and then turn left signposted Blandford. After about a mile the A354 crosses the line of a Roman road and, on the left, you will see Bokerley Ditch. It is possible that this was a barrier, made in the late Roman period, to stop a threatened barbarian invasion of Dorset from the north-east.

After 2 miles turn right along the B3081 signposted Shaftesbury and Sixpenny Handley. Continue over a

crossroads into the village. Sixpenny Handley derives its name from a combination of two ancient districts, Saxpena and Hanlega. **The B3081 turns left past the church and then, at the T-junction, continues right through steep-sided downs to Tollard Royal in the heart of Cranborne Chase.** Apart from King John who hunted there in the thirteenth century and gave the village its royal title, its most famous resident was the archaeologist, General Pitt Rivers. **Just past the village pond there is a parking area on the right.** It is best to leave your car here and walk up the lane on the left signed to the church. After a few yards you will see the gates of King John's House ahead and, beyond them, the half-timbered house dating from the thirteenth century. It was restored in 1889 by General Pitt Rivers and is private.

Return to your car and drive up the lane on the left past the church. Follow the lane to a T-junction and turn left. The road runs past Farnham Woods, a remnant of the great forests that once covered Cranborne Chase. A lane on the left leads to the Larmer Tree Gardens. Open to the public, the gardens take their name from the Larmer Tree, a wych elm, under which it is said King John assembled his huntsmen. This tree has now been replaced by an oak. **When a road joins on the left, continue along the right-hand road signposted Ringwood. Drive straight over a crossroads. The road turns sharp left to a T-junction. Turn right signposted Blandford to meet the A354 where you turn right signposted Blandford and Tarrant Hinton. After about ¼ mile turn right signposted Chettle and Chettle House.** The car park for the house is signed to the left of the road.

Now for a tour of the Tarrants. You need to watch the signposts carefully and take things slowly! **Retrace the route to the A354 and turn right to continue towards Tarrant Hinton. Pass a turning on the right in Tarrant Hinton and, almost immediately, turn left signposted Tarrant Launceston and Tarrant Monkton.** The route now follows the valley of the Tarrant stream through a succession of villages that could have featured in the pages of a Thomas Hardy novel.

Drive through Tarrant Launceston to a T-junction in Tarrant Monkton. Turn left then immediately right signposted Tarrant Rawston. Continue down the valley, keeping to the main road as it bears right beneath a steep hillside and turns right to cross the stream to Tarrant Rawston. Bear left to a Y-junction and continue along the left-hand road for Tarrant Rushton and Tarrant Keyneston. Drive straight over the B3082 signposted Tarrant Crawford. Just past the church in Tarrant Keyneston there is a parking area on the left. From here a walk of about 1/4 mile brings you to a very special place, Tarrant Crawford. The church has retained its fourteenth-century wall paintings, some of which depict the life of St. Margaret of Antioch. The barn behind the church is all that remains of a house for nuns or anchoresses for whom Bishop Richard Poore wrote a rule book in the thirteenth century, the

• PLACES OF INTEREST •

Rockbourne Roman Villa
The villa, discovered in 1942, was one of the largest in southern Britain containing forty-two rooms. The site has been partly backfilled but the outlines of the villa are clearly marked. In the centre the plan of the Iron Age homestead which the villa replaced is laid out in concrete. Interesting features of the villa include two mosaic floors and a unique form of underfloor heating which used curved roof tiles set on end, rather than the usual stacks of bricks.

The museum houses some fascinating exhibits including a third-century New Forest pottery jar filled with 7,717 bronze coins.

Open Good Friday–30 June, Monday–Friday, 2–6. July and August, daily, 10.30–6. 1 September–31 October, weekends, 10.30–6. Telephone: Rockbourne (017253) 541 or 445

Chettle House, near Blandford
This is an interesting small manor designed by Thomas Archer.

The gardens contain many rare chalk-loving plants and some of these are available for sale to visitors. Open 14 April–8 October, daily, 11–5. Closed Tuesday and Saturday. Telephone: Blandford (01258) 830209

Kingston Lacy
The mansion was designed by Sir Roger Pratt for Sir Ralph Bankes and remained the family home until the death of H.J.R. Bankes in 1981. The interior is richly decorated with treasures brought from abroad, including a grand marble staircase from Italy. Paintings feature work by Velazquez, Murillo, Rubens, Van Dyck and Raphael. The estate covers 8,795 acres, offering walks through varied scenery, sometimes along trackways dating from Iron Age, Roman and Saxon times.

Open 1 April–31 October. Park and Gardens 11.30–6. Kingston Lacy House 12–5.30. Closed Thursday and Friday. Telephone: Wimborne (01202) 882493

Ancren Riwle. The ladies, it states, are to live a retired and simple life but are allowed to keep a cat!

Return to your car and keep on towards the Stour valley to a T-junction. Turn left signposted Spetisbury to follow the valley with the river on your right. At the T-junction turn left for Shapwick. Almost immediately the road turns right for Shapwick. At the crossroads in the centre of the village turn left signposted Badbury Rings. The road meets the B3082 opposite the earthwork. Turn right here along the B3082 and, almost immediately on the left, you will see the entrance to the large car park for the Rings. The Iron Age fort dominates the skyline. Two Roman roads from Bath to Poole and from Dorchester to Old Sarum intersected at Badbury.

The tour now follows the B3082 as it runs beneath an avenue of fine beech trees to Wimborne Minster. The entrance to Kingston Lacy, owned by the National Trust, is on the right and a visit to this magnificent mansion concludes the tour. ■

Badbury Rings stands at the intersection of two Roman roads

WAREHAM AND
THE ISLE OF PURBECK

56 MILES – 3 HOURS
START AND FINISH AT WAREHAM

There are many attractions in this tour of the Purbeck Hills which can take a half day or more – the Arne peninsula, Corfe, Studland, the Swanage Steam Railway, Kimmeridge and Lulworth – so it is a good plan to use the route as a 'menu' and choose your favourites! The tour can be used as a guide to a holiday in the Purbecks, with the option of a visit to Brownsea Island.

As the route runs over army training areas near Lulworth look for red warning flags and observe any diversion notices. For information telephone Bindon Abbey (01929) 462721. A small toll is charged at the entrance to Kimmeridge Bay car park.

Leave the centre of Wareham heading south down the main street along the B3075. Cross South Bridge over the River Frome. The road runs through Stoborough over flat watermeadows laced with tiny streams. **Turn left at the crossroads signposted Arne and Ridge. At the next crossroads turn right.** The road runs east towards Poole Harbour over the Arne peninsula, a remote wilderness of heathland dotted with pine woods and the occasional oak copse. The slopes of the Purbeck Hills rise to the south beyond a maze of creeks and inlets. The Royal Society for the Protection of Birds (RSPB) has provided a car park and picnic area not far from the harbour, and from there you can follow a nature trail which leads to a splendid viewpoint at Shipstal Point. **To visit the Purbeck Toy and Musical Box Museum,**

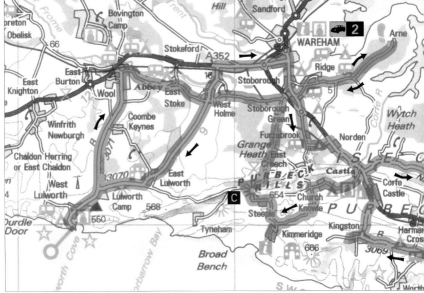

SCALE 1:166 666 OR ABOUT 1 INCH TO 2½ MILES *1 CM TO 1.66 KM*

Wareham

This historic town is situated on a low ridge between the rivers Frome and Piddle commanding the approaches to the Purbeck Hills, Poole Harbour and the east Dorset coast. The town's strategic position and, in earlier times, its usefulness as a cross-channel port made it vulnerable to attack and in 879 it was captured briefly by the Danes. King Alfred fortified the town with walls on three sides. The embankments which supported them, known as Wareham Walls, still surround the town.

St Martin's Church stands on the North Walls. The chancel and nave date from the eleventh century, and there are a series of medieval wall paintings. The church also contains Eric Kennington's effigy of Lawrence of Arabia in Arab dress.

As a result of disastrous fires, the worst being in 1726, Wareham gained many fine Georgian buildings. Particularly fine are the Almshouses on the south side of East Street.

The town lost its usefulness as a port as the River Frome gradually filled with silt, but the quay is still an attractive and busy place. You can take a cruise from here along the river and hire motor and rowing boats from nearby Abbots Quay.

Wareham Museum has a special section devoted to Lawrence of Arabia. Open Easter–mid-October, Monday–Saturday. Telephone: Wareham (01929) 553448

The Purbeck Toy and Musical Box Museum

A delightful journey into the world of toys. Bonzo's tearoom. Opening times vary. Telephone: Wareham (01929) 552018

The Blue Pool, near Wareham

The grounds are open March–November, daily, from 9.30. Tea house, shops and museum open Easter–early October. Telephone: Wareham (01929) 551408

---

continue past the car park and 'no turning past this point' notice. There is free car parking at the Toy Museum for the duration of your visit only.

Retrace the route to Stoborough, turning left at the crossroads to meet the B3075. Turn left signposted Swanage. At the roundabout take the second exit for Furzebrook and the Blue Pool. Drive through Furze-brook village and turn left following the Blue Pool signs to a car park. The Blue Pool was originally a clay pit, and the diffraction of light from particles of clay in the water creates an amazing illusion of colour. It is surrounded by twenty-five acres of heathland and pine woods where paths lead down to the water's edge.

The exit road from the car park leads to the A351. **Turn right for Corfe.** Ahead, commanding a gap in the Purbeck Hills, rise the ruins of Corfe Castle. **Drive up to the Square in Corfe village and turn right following the car park sign. Turn right to enter the large** car park. Corfe village has been described as 'a symphony in grey'. All the cottages are built and roofed with the local grey stone softened by ferns and climbing plants. Although ruined, the castle still retains the romantic appeal of turrets scaled by twisting stairs, dungeons and battlemented walkways.

To continue the tour return to the square, turn left and then take the first road on the right under the railway bridge signposted Studland, the B3351. After 3 miles a parking area on the left gives beautiful views north over Poole Harbour. **At the crossroads in Studland village be ready to**

An astonishing effect of colour is created in the deep-blue waters of the Blue Pool near Wareham

19

Impressive Norman architecture can be seen in Studland Church

turn right **A** in front of the newsagents, Studland Stores. **Keep to the same road as it turns left (past a no-through road sign) to the church.** There is roadside parking here. The Norman Church of St Nicholas is one of the finest in Dorset. The huge Norman arches of the chancel are supported by carved pillars, and the groined and vaulted roofs of the chancel and sanctuary are superb.

Return down the lane from the church and turn left signposted to the beach. If you wish to visit the beach there is a National Trust car park on the right. Studland Bay offers safe bathing from almost 3 miles of sandy beach sheltered by rising heathland and pine woods. **With the car park on your right continue to a T-junction.** The beach is also accessible from the car park you will see down the road on the left. **To continue the tour, turn left at the T-junction to meet the B3351. Turn right signposted Poole and Bournemouth.** The road now runs north over Studland Heath, a National Nature Reserve. Car parks on the right give access to nature trails. The Purbeck heaths are a refuge for rare wildlife including Dartford warblers, smooth snakes, sand lizards and the lovely silver-studded blue butterfly. Vehicle ferries run from the northern tip of Studland Heath (Shell Bay) across the mouth of Poole Harbour to Sandbanks. The

ferry from Sandbanks to Brownsea Island (10–20 minutes) is for foot passengers only. So, if you wish to visit Brownsea, leave your car in the car park near the ferry at Shell Bay.

Retrace the route to Studland village continuing along the B3351 for about a mile. Turn left signposted

Swanage. The road runs along the valley then bears left through a gap in the hills. **Follow the signs to the sea to run down to the seafront of this pleasant little town.** The sandy bay is just as Thomas Hardy describes it, 'lying snug within two headlands as between a finger and thumb'. The headlands are Ballard Point to the north and the chalk outcrop of Peveril Point to the south. **Look carefully for a small clock tower inland of a small pier on the left. Turn right in front of this clock tower into Victoria Road **B**. This is the A351 but there is no sign.** If you would like a nostalgic trip back in time, steam trains run from Swanage station to Corfe. **Turn left following the sign for the steam train.** The station is on your right and there is a car park but, as this is limited to two hours, you may prefer to use one

---

• *PLACES OF INTEREST* •

Corfe Castle
The ruins date from the time of William the Conqueror, but the Saxon kings had previously fortified the site. Outside the gate the beautiful Saxon queen, Elfrida, poisoned and stabbed her stepson King Edward. Under King John it became a royal residence, a treasure house and a prison.

During the Civil War the castle stood for the King and was heroically defended by Lady Bankes and a small garrison. All efforts to take the castle proved ineffectual until a member of the garrison, Colonel Pitman, let the enemy in. Lady Bankes' bravery won the respect of the Parliamentary forces and she was well treated, but the castle was slighted soon after its capture. Open daily.

Brownsea Island
The island is an enchanting blend of heath and woodland. Guided tours can be taken around the nature reserve, but outside the reserve there are peacocks, exotic pheasants and red squirrels. Wild

geese haunt the shoreline. Restaurant by the quay.

Swanage Steam Railway
Volunteers have restored part of the Swanage to Wareham railway, and you can now enjoy a ride lasting about an hour through the beautiful Purbeck countryside.

Days in steam vary so, for up-to-the-minute information, telephone the 24-hour talking timetable on Wareham (01929) 424276

Lulworth Castle
The castle was built for Thomas Howard, third Lord Bindon. In the eighteenth century it passed to the Weld family who transformed the interior into a gracious country house. Although referred to as a castle it was never intended to be used for military purposes. There was a disastrous fire in 1929 and some years later, in 1984, English Heritage commenced restoration.

Open 30 March–31 October, daily, 10–6. 1 November– 22 December 10–4. Telephone: Wareham (01929) 41352

Lulworth Cove forms a perfect horseshoe and is a favourite with holiday-makers. Visit out of season if you can.

of the town's long stay car parks a few minutes away.

Return to the A351 and turn left to continue west. After about 1½ miles leave the A351 and bear left along the B3069 for Langton Matravers. Behind the church in the centre of Langton Matravers you will find a museum (with free car park) telling the story of the quarrying and use of Purbeck stone. It explains the unique geology of the various 'beds', the topmost layer forming the famous 'Purbeck Marble' which has been cut and polished since Roman times.

Continue to Kingston, an old-world village giving glorious views. As you enter the village leave the B3069 which turns right for Corfe and continue up the village street past the church. Keep ahead along the lane to a car park signed off the road among the trees on the left. From here walks lead seawards along the crest of the downs.

Drive back to the B3069 to meet the A351. Turn left for Corfe. Drive through the village and, at the foot of the hill, turn left signposted Steeple and Kimmeridge. Drive through Church Knowle and, after 2 miles, turn left signposted Kimmeridge. Follow the lane running between the thatched cottages of Kimmeridge village. The bay is famous for fossils and remnants of artefacts made from 'Kimmeridge coal', a band of bituminous shale exposed on the cliff face mined and worked since the Iron Age.

Retrace the route through Kimmeridge village to a T-junction (where you turned left for Kimmeridge) and turn left signposted Steeple and Lulworth. Past Steeple the road climbs the downs then turns sharply right signposted Wareham C to a car park and a magnificent viewpoint on the right. The road runs north through woodlands.

After about 3 miles turn left signposted East and West Lulworth. At the crossroads in West Holme turn left for the Lulworths along the B3070. When the road divides take the right-hand road (B3070) through East Lulworth to a T-junction. Turn right for West Lulworth. On the right is the entrance to Lulworth Castle, a splendid early seventeenth-century building open to the public. **At the junction with the B3071 turn left, still on the B3070, for West Lulworth. Drive down to the car park and museum close to the cove.** The cove is justly famous for its perfect horseshoe shape framed by spectacular cliffs.

Retrace the route along the B3070 through West Lulworth. At the junction with the B3071 do not turn for East Lulworth but continue north for Wool along the B3071. Drive into Wool and at the T-junction take the road on the right signposted Bindon Abbey. Follow the lane as far as the West Holme crossroads and turn left along the B3070 to cross the River Frome. A fine old bridge carries an earlier road over the river, and there is room to pull off onto the old road by the bridge to admire its graceful construction. **Turn right along the A352 for Wareham. At the roundabout continue along the B3070 to the centre of the town.** ■

Swanage Steam Railway now runs from Swanage to Norden, near Corfe

DORCHESTER AND THE HEART OF THOMAS HARDY'S WESSEX

60 MILES – 3 HOURS
START AND FINISH AT DORCHESTER

All readers of Thomas Hardy's novels will recognise the countryside traced in this tour. It includes visits to the thatched cottage at Higher Bockhampton, where he was born and wrote his early novels, and the villa at Max Gate, where he wrote his later works. But there is a great deal more to enjoy in this tour such as Bovington Tank Museum, Lawrence of Arabia's retreat Clouds Hill, the beautiful churches at Moreton and Puddletown, and one of the finest of Dorset's stately homes, Athelhampton.

The cob-and-thatch cottage at Higher Bockhampton where Thomas Hardy was born in 1840 and where he wrote his early novels

From Dorchester's Top o'Town roundabout drive east down the High Street signposted Poole and Blandford. Cross Town Bridge over the River Frome. At the roundabout go over the A35 and take the next road on the left signposted Stinsford. After a few yards turn right to a car park on the left for Stinsford Church. Turn left to walk down to this small grey church in the meadows beside the River Frome. For Hardy this churchyard, where his parents were buried, was 'the dearest spot on earth'. He wished to be buried there also and, although his ashes were interred with honour in Westminster Abbey, his heart was placed in the grave of his first wife, Emma Lavinia Gifford, which is to the left of the path as you enter the churchyard. Stinsford is 'Mellstock' in Hardy's first successful novel *Under the Greenwood Tree*.

From the car park turn right to retrace the route to a T-junction, then turn right. At the crossroads turn left. In 1/2 mile turn right signposted Hardy's Cottage and turn right to the car park at Thorncombe Wood. A short waymarked walk through the woods leads to the cottage. In 1840 Hardy was born in this homely thatched cottage in the Frome valley, overshadowed by the brooding presence of the wild heathland he was to immortalise as 'Egdon'. In *Under the Greenwood Tree* Hardy rents it temporarily to the Dewy family. The hero of the novel, Dick Dewy, follows the novelist's own boyhood walks to church in Stinsford and to the little village school at Lower Bockhampton.

Retrace the route to the lane and turn left. Go straight over the crossroads signposted Lower Bockhampton and continue through this attractive village over the winding rivulets of the River Frome to a T-junction. Turn

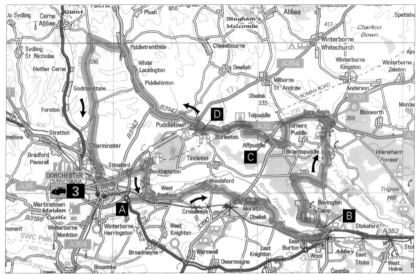

right signposted Dorchester. At the next T-junction turn right again signposted Dorchester. The lane runs to meet the A352. Turn right once more for Dorchester. At the next roundabout ignore the first left turn for Poole and the second left turn for Dorchester. Take the next road on the left (marked no through road) signposted Max Gate **A**. Almost immediately turn left again to follow the old road past the entrance to Max Gate to a parking area on the left. Hardy designed the red brick Victorian villa himself and moved in with his wife in June 1885. Here he wrote his later novels including *The Woodlanders*, *Tess of the d'Urbervilles* and *Jude the Obscure*.

• PLACES OF INTEREST •

Dorchester

In his novel *The Mayor of Casterbridge* Thomas Hardy describes Dorchester (which he renames 'Casterbridge') as appearing 'compact as a box of dominoes'. Today, the centre of this small county town is still confined within the embankments of its Roman walls, and meadows fringe the foot of High East Street. The Romans founded Dorchester as *Durnovaria* and established a military tradition still important today.

Behind the County Hall the remains of a fine Roman villa, complete with hypercausts and mosaics, has been excavated. The court room in Shire Hall, where the Tolpuddle Martyrs were convicted, is now owned by the TUC and is open to the public. St Peters Church, dating from the fifteenth century, overlooks the town pump where the hiring fairs were once held, and outside is a statue of Dorset's dialect poet, William Barnes. There is a

memorial statue of Thomas Hardy near the roundabout at the top of High West Street.

Dorchester has always been an important meeting place, market and economic centre, a position it still holds. The town has a large livestock market, a brewery and other light industries. Market day is Wednesday.

Dorchester's history can be explored in the excellent **County Museum** in High West Street.

Fascinating displays include a reconstruction of Hardy's study at Max Gate. Open Monday–Saturday, 10–5 and, in July and August, Sunday, 10–5. Telephone: Dorchester (01305) 262735

Max Gate This house is preserved as it was in Hardy's time, but the furnishings of his study have been assembled in Dorchester Museum. A visitor to Max Gate in 1886 described the house as 'an unpretending red-brick structure of moderate size, somewhat quaintly built'. He was greeted by the frenzied barking of Hardy's black setter, Moss, whose grave is in the garden. Open March–September, Sunday, Monday and Wednesday afternoons, 2–5. Telephone: (01305) 262538

The Keep Military Museum celebrates 300 years of military history. Open Monday–Saturday 9.30–5. Telephone: (01305) 264066

23

Stinsford Church, the 'Mellstock' of Thomas Hardy's novel Under the Greenwood Tree

Facing the entrance to Max Gate, turn right from the parking area past the blue West Stafford Cycleway sign and turn left to the A352. Turn left to the next roundabout and then left again signposted West Stafford (retracing the earlier route). After 3/4 mile turn left signposted Lower Bockhampton. After 1/4 mile leave the earlier route and turn right signposted West Stafford. The road curves right to a T-junction in West Stafford village. Turn left past the church. The church was probably the scene of Tess's marriage to Angel Clare in *Tess of the d'Urbervilles*. This lush valley of the River Frome was the setting for Talbothays Farm where she worked as a dairymaid.

Follow the lane to the next T-junction and turn left signposted Woodsford. At the Y-junction take the left-hand road signposted Woodsford. You will pass Woodsford Castle, now a farm. Dating from the early fourteenth century it is probably one of the oldest inhabited buildings in England.

Keep ahead, signposted Moreton, to cross the B3390. At the T-junction in the village turn left to the riverside parking area. Walk back up the lane and turn left past the Moreton Estate sign to see the

church. This beautiful church, with its magnificent sequence of engraved glass windows designed by Laurence Whistler, is a 'must' on this tour. Lawrence of Arabia is buried in the churchyard and to see his grave return to the road and turn left – the cemetery is on the right.

To continue the tour drive back to the road and turn left signposted East Burton and Wool. The road follows the Frome valley. Continue over the crossroads in East Burton to meet the A352 in Wool. Turn left along the A352 signposted Wareham for just a few yards and then take the minor road on the left signposted Woolbridge. Cross Wool Bridge over the River Frome. On the left is the Jacobean manor house where Tess and Angel Clare spent their ill-fated honeymoon.

At the T-junction turn left to run up to a Y-junction **B**. The route turns left here, but you might like to make a short detour along the right-hand road to visit Monkey World. If so, after your visit, retrace your route to **B** and take the road signposted Bovington. Bovington Tank Museum is on the right. The road rises between the forested slopes of Hardy's 'Egdon', once bleak heathland and the setting for *The Return of the Native*. The car park for

Lawrence of Arabia's cottage, Clouds Hill, is on the right.

Turn right at the T-junction signposted Bere Regis to cross Wool Heath. At the next T-junction turn left signposted Bere Regis. There is a picnic area on the left. As you approach the village, Hardy's Kingsbere-sub-Greenhill, you will see trenches and embankments in a field on the right. These are the foundations of a palace built by King John in 1205. Turn left following the signs to the car park to visit Bere Regis church. The carved wood roof of the nave, with its figures of the twelve Apostles dressed as Tudor gentlemen, was the gift of Cardinal Morton, later Lord Chancellor of England, who was born in Bere Regis in 1425. In *Tess of the d'Urbervilles* Bere Regis is the home of Tess's ancestors. When evicted from their cottage, Tess's mother, Joan, sets the family bedstead by the south wall under the Turberville window claiming that their family vault is their own freehold. The beautiful window is to the right of the south porch.

Turn left from the entrance to the car park and then left again through the village to meet the A35. Continue along the A35 following the signs for Tolpuddle and Puddletown. Turn left signposted Briantspuddle. You will now see some of the

One of the exquisite engraved windows in Moreton Church

charming villages in the Puddle valley. The river is called the Puddle as far as Puddletown, then it becomes the Piddle! **At the crossroads in Briantspuddle turn right signposted Affpuddle to meet the B3390 and continue for Affpuddle. When the B3390 turns right signposted Bere Regis C leave the B3390 and bear a little left to continue past the church in Affpuddle. Keep to the lane as it turns right to Tolpuddle.** On the left is the sycamore under which the famous Tolpuddle martyrs held their meetings. Driven by poverty they formed a union and were arrested for swearing illegal oaths. Sentenced to be transported they were able to return to Dorset after some years. **At the junction with the A35 turn left signposted Dorchester and Puddletown.** You will pass the TUC (Trades Union Congress) Memorial Cottages Museum on the right. **Continue towards Puddletown.** On the right is the entrance to Athelhampton House, a fifteenth-century mansion surrounded by a series of 'secret' gardens.

The village of Puddletown is the 'Weatherbury' of Hardy's *Far from the Madding Crowd*. **To see the church, which figures so prominently in the novel, turn right into the village opposite the bus shelter past the book shop, signed for Ilsington House D. Turn right to the church where there is room to park.** Hardy brought his friend Gustav Holst to see the magnificent oak gallery dated 1635. Inside the box pew to the left of the gallery steps you will see 'Henery' carved with an extra 'e', a detail which prompted Hardy to call one of the characters in his novel 'Henery' Fray.

With the church on your left turn right and then left to meet the A354. Turn right for just a few yards, then left along the B3142 signposted

Hardy's Cottage, Higher Bockhampton
The cottage remains very much as it was in Hardy's time. The exterior can be viewed 1 April–31 October, daily except Thursday, 11–6. To view the interior make an appointment either by letter (Hardy's Cottage, Higher Bockhampton, Dorchester, Dorset) or by telephone: Dorchester (01305) 262366

Monkey World, near Wool
This refuge for primates was started in 1985 to rescue chimpanzees from Spanish beach photographers and provide them with a natural, stable environment. At present there are fifteen chimpanzees, two orang-utans, a group of Barbary apes, several species of lemur and families of macaques. Picnic areas, refreshments, shop. Open every day except Christmas and New Year, 10–5 (later during peak season). Telephone: Bindon Abbey (01929) 462537

Bovington Tank Museum
The museum contains tanks and armoured cars from all parts of the world, many in exciting diorama settings. There are two driver simulators, a guided missile simulator and two video theatres. Picnic areas, shop, refreshments. Open daily, 10–5. Closed for ten days at Christmas.

Telephone: Bindon Abbey (01929) 462721 extension 3463 or 3329
    The museum features a permanent 'Lawrence of Arabia' exhibition and offers research facilities. The library is open weekdays, 10–1, 2–4.30. Appointments are preferred. Telephone: Bindon Abbey (01929) 462721 extension 3463

Clouds Hill, Bovington
This simple brick and tiled cottage became the retreat of Lawrence of Arabia from 1923 until his death in 1935. The cottage is as he left it. Open 22 April–29 October Wednesday, Thursday, Friday and Sunday, 2–5.

Athelhampton House and Gardens, Puddletown
A lived-in family house with a magnificent Great Hall and Great Chamber. Refreshments, shop. Open 2 April–29 October, Tuesday, Wednesday, Thursday, Sunday and Bank Holidays, 12–5. Telephone: Dorchester (01305) 848363

Ilsington House, Puddletown
Step back into the eighteenth century in this elegant Georgian house. Open Wednesday and Thursday, 2–6. Also Sunday in August. Telephone: Dorchester (01305) 848454

Piddletrenthide, Druce and Waterston to follow the banks of the River Piddle. All the farming scenes in *Far from the Madding Crowd* are set in this valley. **Keep to the main road as it bears left to cross the stream.** Druce Farm on the right is the original of Farmer Boldwood's house in the novel.

Drive through the tiny hamlet of Lower Waterston. On the right high hedges surround the Jacobean mansion, Bathsheba Everdene's home in the novel. **When the B3142 meets the B3143 at a T-junction turn right signposted Piddle-**

trenthide and Sturminster Newton. Keep to the main road as it follows the Piddle valley through Piddlehinton to Piddletrenthide. Turn left in this village signposted Cerne Abbas. The lane divides before a T-junction. Turn left at the T-junction signposted Dorchester. Now you can enjoy magnificent views over the countryside where Gabriel Oak pastured his sheep in *Far from the Madding Crowd*. **The road runs high above the downs for over 5 miles to Dorchester and the Top o'Town roundabout.** ■

25

MAIDEN CASTLE, ABBOTSBURY AND PORTLAND

59 MILES – 3 HOURS
START AND FINISH AT DORCHESTER

An exploration of Dorset's most impressive hill-fort, Maiden Castle, begins this tour. There are spectacular views as the route runs to the coast at Abbotsbury, famous for its swannery. Readers of Meade Falkner's novel Moonfleet *will be intrigued by a visit to the ruined church of the Mohuns which inspired the book. The tour also includes a visit to Portland, a place with a unique character. More magnificent views can be enjoyed as the route returns to Dorchester via Weymouth.*

The tour starts from Dorchester's Top o'Town roundabout at the top of High West Street. Take the A354 heading south, signposted Weymouth. Keep to the main road as it turns right at a junction signposted All Routes to cross the railway. In ¼ mile turn right along a minor road signposted Maiden Castle. The road bridges the A35 and continues to a car park. Footpaths scale the ramparts of Maiden Castle, the largest of Dorset's hill-forts, encircling forty-six acres.

Retrace the route to the A354 (B3157). Turn right and, at the second round-about, keep straight on along the A354. This ruler-straight road, following the line of a Roman road, leads over Ridgeway Hill. **A dog-leg takes the road over and under the railway. After ½ mile turn right along the B3159 signposted Winter-bourne Abbas. Keep to the main road as it bears right to Upwey.** This pretty village is tucked neatly in a wooded cleft of the downs. A car park is signed to the left of the road. Close by is the Upwey Wishing Well and a picturesque mill. The novelist Thomas Hardy had the mill in mind as the home of Anne Garland in *The Trumpet-Major*.

Turn left from the car park in Upwey to continue north along the B3159. The road climbs the downs to a T-junction at Martinstown. **Turn left continuing along the B3159.** The little Winterborne stream runs beside the road as you drive through this attractive village. **At a T-junction leave the B3159 and turn left along the lane signposted Hardy's Monument and Portesham.** The lane winds over the downs towards the monument on the highest point of Black Down Hill. **Pass the monument on the left and turn left into the car park.** The 70-foot- (21 metres) high monument was erected on this old beacon hill in memory of Thomas Masterman Hardy, Captain of Nelson's flagship HMS *Victory* at the battle of Trafalgar. It affords a magnificent view of the seas he fought so hard to defend. From west to east it is possible to trace the coast from Start Point in Devon to the Needles off the Isle of Wight. Ahead lies Portland which, in the novelist Thomas Hardy's words, resembled 'a great crouching animal tethered to the mainland'.

With the monument on your left, continue to a cross-roads. Turn left signposted Portesham to descend steeply into the village. The road bears left through the village to meet the B3157. Bear right

Dorset's greatest hill-fort, Maiden Castle

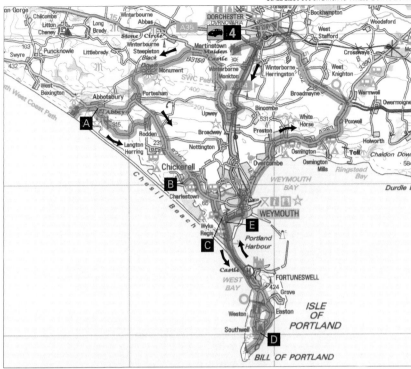

• PLACES OF INTEREST •

Maiden Castle
This huge hill-fort dominates the skyline south-west of Dorchester. Men of the New Stone Age were the first to settle here. Extensive fortifications, including stone walling, were made by early Iron Age tribes who set up farming communities and manufactured and traded cloth. The small town grew into the major stronghold of the Durotriges. New methods of warfare, including the use of the sling as a weapon, reinforced their security. But, in AD 44 the fort proved no match for the might of Rome. The 2nd Augusta Legion, led by Vespasian, attacked the more vulnerable eastern gate and, after fierce fighting, the fort was taken. Occupation of the site gradually ceased except for the building of a Romano-British temple in the fourth century AD.

Abbotsbury
The Swannery For over 600 years a colony of swans has made its home on the Fleet at Abbotsbury. The swans are first mentioned in the Benedictine Monks' Court Rolls in 1393. The monks, the ruins of whose monastery are close by, found the swans a useful source of fresh meat, quills for writing and down for pillows.
Visitors can stroll along the walkways and mingle with the swans, even help to feed them. Open 5 March–29 October, every day, 10–6. Telephone: Weymouth (01305) 871684

The Tithe Barn Museum
This fifteenth-century barn brings the past to life with a display of rural bygones. Telephone: (01305) 871817/852

The Sub-Tropical Gardens
Rare plants from all over the world flourish in these wonderful gardens. There is a tea garden and plant shop. Open March–October, every day, 10–6. Rest of the year 10–4. Telephone: (01305) 871387

signposted Abbotsbury. On the right is Portesham House, the boyhood home of Captain Hardy. Two stone lions mount guard over the front porch. In *The Trumpet-Major* Bob Loveday calls at the house anxious to have the opportunity to fight on board HMS *Victory*.

Follow the B3157 to the old-world village of Abbotsbury. Framed by the downs, a long street of stone-built thatched cottages stands close to the placid waters of the Fleet protected by the pebble bank of Chesil Beach. There is a car park on the left as you enter the village. From here you can see the remains of St Peter's Abbey, walk to the magnificent Tithe Barn and, if you wish, follow a footpath to the famous Swannery. **If you prefer to motor, drive through the village and take the next road on the left past the Ilchester Arms A.** The lane leads down to the car park for the Swannery. A footpath from a lane just past the Ilchester Arms leads uphill to the fifteenth-century Chapel

27

The Swannery, Abbotsbury. This is a 'must' for all visitors to Dorset.

of St Catherine. Abbotsbury is also famous for its sub-tropical gardens. **To visit them continue west along the B3157 and turn left following the sign for the gardens and the car park.**

The tour continues from **A**. Follow the signs for Abbotsbury Swannery. Keep to the lane past the car park as it bears right to run through the strangely remote world hidden behind the low ridge of downland fronting the Fleet.

Drive through Rodden to a T-junction and turn right signposted Weymouth along the B3157. Continue for about 3¹/₂ miles. At a round-about, when the main road turns left, keep straight on down the lane ahead sign-posted East Fleet. The road runs towards the sea then bears right **B**. When you see a large church on the right, turn right into the churchyard where parking is permitted. To see the church of the Mohuns walk back up the road to **B**. Turn right past a row of cottages (Butterstreet) and go through the small iron gate. Only the chancel of the old church survived the disastrous storm of 23 November 1824, when great waves pounded over Chesil Beach. Inside there is a memorial plaque to John Meade Falkner.

Retrace the route to the B3157 and turn right for Weymouth and Portland.

After 1¹/₂ miles bear right along the B3156 (A354) signposted Portland. The B3156 turns left for just a few yards to pass a turning on the right. Turn right down the next turning **C** sign-posted Portland to meet the A354. Follow the A354 along

the Chesil Bank towards the village of Fortuneswell on Portland. At the roundabout keep to the A354 following the signs for Through Traffic. The road climbs through Fortuneswell then snakes up the steep hillside called, by Thomas Hardy, 'the massive forehead of the Isle'. Stop in the car park on the top and walk to the War Memorial for one of the finest views in Wessex. At your feet the Dorset coast is spread like a map – westward runs the long ridge of the Chesil Bank reaching Abbotsbury, trapping behind it the waters of the Fleet, and to the east sweeps the gentle curve of Weymouth Bay.

Keep to the main road to continue to Easton. At the T-junction in Easton turn left along Straits Road signposted

---

• PLACES OF INTEREST •

Portland
The Royal Manor of Portland is quite unlike any other part of Wessex. During the Middle Ages the people lived remote from the mainland on their almost treeless rocky outpost, smuggling, fishing and grazing a unique brand of sheep. They had their own parliament and made their own laws. They were adept with the sling, giving rise to Thomas Hardy's name for their home 'the Isle of Slingers'. Some of that sense of mystery remains today.

The excellence of Portland stone was recognised after the Great Fire of London, first by Inigo Jones who built the Banqueting House, Whitehall, and later by Sir Christopher Wren who used the stone for the new St Paul's and other city churches.

In 1847 the Government decided to establish a naval base on the island and a prison to house a labour force for the quarries. Although not pic-turesque in the conventional sense the island offers cliff walks with magnificent views.

The Portland Museum consists of two converted houses,

217 Wakeham and 'Avice Cottage'. Picnic area, gift shop. Open daily, 10.30–1, 1.30–5.

Weymouth
In 1789 this small town, situated on a beautiful bay of gently shelving sand, became famous almost overnight with the visit of George III and his family to try the newly-discovered delights of sea bathing. An Esplanade was built backed by elegant Georgian terraces. There is also 'old' Weymouth, a pleasing blend of narrow streets and seventeenth-century cottages.

Details of the resort's many attractions can be obtained from the Tourist Information Office, but not to be missed are:
The Timewalk Exhibition set in the old Devenish Brewery on Brewer's Quay. Open all year, daily, 9.30–5.30 (9.30 pm during summer holidays) Telephone: Weymouth (01305) 777622
Nothe Fort overlooking the Old Harbour. Open 5 May– 24 September, daily, from 10.30. Telephone: Weymouth (01305) 787243

Portland Bill. At the cross roads turn right into Wakeham. This wide street has many houses built and roofed with stone with tiny stone porches. On the left, on the corner of a narrow lane leading down to Church Ope Cove, is the Portland Museum and 'Avice Cottage'. The cottage is the Caros' home in Hardy's novel *The Well-Beloved*. Follow the main road a few yards further as it bears right to a car park on the right. Walk back to the lane to visit the Museum and 'Avice Cottage'. The lane leads to a footpath to the cove past the ruined keep of the twelfth-century Rufus Castle. Close to the beach are the ruins of St Andrew's Church, the parish church of Portland until 1756.

From the car park turn right to continue the tour following the signs for Portland Bill. Turn left in Southwell signposted Portland Bill D. The road leads to a car park close to the southern tip of the island and the Bird Observatory. A footpath leads to Pulpit Rock confronting the infamous Portland Race. Retrace the route to the T-junction at D and turn left.

The road curves right through Southwell and Weston. Bear left following the signs for Weymouth. Turn left again along the A354 for Weymouth. Follow the one-way system through Fortuneswell and retrace the route along the Chesil Bank. Cross Ferry Bridge and continue for about ¾ mile through Wyke Regis. Keep to the A354 as it turns right signposted Dorchester E.

The A354 turns left to run up to a roundabout by the yacht harbour. Bear left here signposted Dorchester. The road follows the waterside to another roundabout. Bear right along the A353 signposted Wareham to cross the estuary of the River Wey. At the roundabout continue along the A353 signposted Wareham to the seafront of Weymouth Bay. Turn left and follow the A353 as it curves around the bay. Keep to the main road as it turns inland for a few yards before returning to the coast again. Lodmoor Nature Reserve with ample parking is on the left.

Keep to the A353 following the signs for Wareham as it turns inland and then bears right through Preston. In ¾ mile a road leads left to one of the most picturesque villages in Dorset, Sutton Poyntz. A cluster of old cottages surround a mill beside an overflowing pond complete with friendly ducks. Parking is limited in the village, so it is better to park by the church and walk the ¼ mile into the village. The church car park is a few yards down the lane on the right, opposite the turning to Sutton Poyntz.

Return to your car and keep on along the A353. The white figure of George III is carved out of the downland turf on the left. Keep to the A353 as it bears left to meet the A352. Turn left signposted Dorchester and bear left for Dorchester at the first roundabout. At the next roundabout keep ahead still following the sign for Dorchester. Keep straight on at the next roundabout signed Town Centre. At the T-junction turn right to meet the B3150 by Grey's Bridge. Turn left to drive up Dorchester High Street to Top o'Town roundabout. ■

George III's visits made Weymouth a popular resort. He is commemorated by this white figure carved out of the turf on the hillside north of Osmington.

BLANDFORD FORUM AND THE NORTH DORSET DOWNS

50 MILES – 3 HOURS
START AND FINISH AT BLANDFORD FORUM

Magnificent views from some of Dorset's highest hills, including a splendid panorama of the Blackmoor Vale from the top of Bulbarrow, feature in this tour. And there is much else to enjoy. The route runs through valleys carved by chalk streams and across the undulating meadowland of the Blackmoor Vale to hidden villages where time seems to have stood still. A highlight of the return route is a visit to historic Milton Abbey.

Leaflets giving details of the walks in this tour are available from the Tourist Information Office in Blandford.

Leave the centre of Blandford Forum heading north following the sign for Warminster and the A354 (A350). At the Y-junction take the left-hand road. The road dips along the east bank of the River Stour then meets the A350. Turn left signed Warminster. Beautiful views of pastoral countryside framed by gently curving hills open ahead. **Continue along the A350 past the junction with the A357 to run through Stourpaine.** The route now continues north beside the little River Iwerne. Rising to the left, protected to the west by the River Stour and to the east by the River

Iwerne, is Hod Hill. Excavations on the summit in the 1950s revealed the embankments and hut circles of a fifty-four-acre Iron Age hill-fort, possibly destroyed by the Romans who built a fort in the north-west corner of the site around AD 45–63.

The A350 curves left to cross the River Iwerne. Pass a turning on the left for Child Okeford and take the next turning on the left signposted Shroton (Iwerne Courtney). This attractive village of thatched stone and brick cottages lies on the lower slopes of Hambledon Hill. You may wish to stop here and take a walk of just over

¹/₂ mile to the top of the hill. The grassy summit is deeply scored by the embankments of another Iron Age fort and the view is one of the finest in Dorset. Opposite the church there is a parking area to the right of the road. With the church on your left, walk down the road and turn left down Fairfield Road. After about 100 yards (92 metres) a sign on the left indicates a footpath leading uphill. When this divides follow the right-hand path to the summit.

To continue the tour drive through Iwerne Courtney to the T-junction and turn right down Frog Lane to rejoin the A350. Turn left to head north again for Iwerne Minster, a charming old-world village. The church has a medieval stone spire – a distinction shared with only two other Dorset churches at Winterbourne Steepleton and Trent.

Keep ahead along the A350 to Fontmell Magna. At the crossroads in the village leave the A350 and turn left . Drive straight over the next crossroads to head west for Bedchester. After a mile

Elegant classical architecture is a feature of Blandford Forum

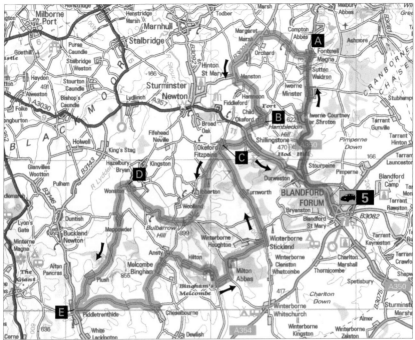

drive over the Bedchester
crossroads. The road climbs a
little then swings round a corner
to give a magnificent view over
the Blackmoor Vale. **After
dropping into the vale, the
road runs to meet the B3091
at a multiple junction. Drive
across the junction (beware
traffic precedence!) to join
the B3091 signposted
Sturminster and Manston.
Keep to the main road as
it bears left to Manston.**

**In Manston the B3091
turns right. Leave the main
road and bear a little left
signposted Child Okeford.
As you enter Child Okeford
village you will pass a joining
road on the left. Drive past
the church, village shop and
Post Office, and be ready to
take the next road on the
right – Station Road – the
sign for Shillingstone is
above the road name** B.

The road runs through water-
meadows to cross the River Stour.
**Continue under a railway
bridge to meet the the the
A357. Turn left signposted
Durweston and Blandford**

• PLACES OF INTEREST •

Blandford Forum

The small market town of
Blandford Forum is beautifully
situated in the valley of the River
Stour framed by wooded hillsides.
The town developed at the point
where several ancient routes
converged to cross the river, first
by ford then by bridges. By the
fourteenth century the town was
important enough to send two
members to Parliament. This
prosperity came to an abrupt end
in 1731 when almost all the town
was destroyed by fire. Rebuilding
was entrusted to William and John
Bastard who were civic dignitaries
and architect-surveyors. They did
their work well, and today
Blandford Forum has the most
perfect and satisfying Georgian
red brick and stone town centre
in the south-west.

Dominating the market-place
is the tower and cupola of
Blandford Church. The fine
interior contains massive Portland
stone columns. The pulpit, the
work of Sir Christopher Wren,
came from St Antholin's Church
in the City of London. Perhaps the
grandest of the Georgian secular
buildings is Coupar House, at the
top of Church Lane.

The town provides a market
and meeting place for the rich
farming countryside of the Stour
valley. It is also well known for
the production of beer.

Blandford Museum, off the
Market Place houses displays
illustrating the life, culture and
industry of the town. It has a
gallery named after the artist
Alfred Stevens who was born
in Blandford and whose most
famous work is the memorial
to the Duke of Wellington in
St Paul's. Open 1 April–late
September, Tuesday–Saturday,
10–4.

The Royal Signals Museum
is 2 miles north-east of the town.
It contains items dealing with the
history of army communications
from the Crimean War to the
Gulf War. Open all year, Monday–
Friday, 10–5, and June–
September, Saturday and
Sunday, 10–4. Telephone:
Blandford (01258) 482248

31

Okeford Fitzpaine, one of Dorset's most attractive villages with many half-timbered and thatched cottages

to drive into Shillingstone village. Opposite the school leave the A357 and turn right signposted Okeford Fitzpaine. The road bends left then right past the church in Okeford Fitzpaine to a Y-junction. Bear left signed for Ibberton then, at the T-junction, turn left **C**. Okeford Fitzpaine is a beautiful village and, if you would like to spend a little time there, turn right where you will find off-road parking. Now a conservation area, the village was described by the historian Frederick Treves as 'a part of the Dorset of old days'.

Shortly after leaving the village take the right-hand road at a junction signposted Woolland. The steep slopes of the north Dorset downs rise ahead as the road runs to a Y-junction. Turn left signposted Ansty and Bulbarrow to climb the side of Ibberton Hill. The road now follows the ridge of Woolland Down and Bulbarrow Hill for 2 miles giving spectacular views over the Blackmoor Vale. Perhaps the finest views are from Bulbarrow car park which is on the left of the road. Bulbarrow was one of Thomas Hardy's favourite Wessex

heights. The Blackmoor Vale, his 'vale of little dairies', is Tess's home in *Tess of the d'Urbervilles*. A world of small thickly-hedged fields, copses and low wooded slopes lies at your feet stretching to a horizon fringed by the Blackdown and Quantock hills. On a clear day you may glimpse the silver gleam of the Severn estuary far away to the north-west.

Continue along the ridge, bear right, and then right again signposted Mappowder and Stoke Wake. Pass the embankments of Rawlsbury hill-fort to run downhill into Stoke Wake. When the road divides keep ahead for Hazelbury Bryan. At the T-junction turn right in the direction of Hazelbury Bryan. Just south of the village the road runs to a T-junction in Wonston. Turn left to drive past a lane with a no-through-road sign. Take the next unsigned road on the left – it is just past a telephone kiosk **D**. Almost immediately turn left again. The road bears left to run south to Mappowder.

Approaching the village the road divides. Take the right-hand road signposted Folly, Plush and Piddletrenthide.

The road climbs the downs again in the shadow of Nettlecombe Tout. Continue through Folly for Plush, a small settlement sandwiched between steep-sided downs. The road descends through woods into the valley of the River Piddle to meet the B3143 opposite the fine eighteenth-century manor in Piddletrenthide. Turn left along the B3143 for only a few yards then take the next road on the left signposted Doles Ash and Ch. (Cheselbourne) Bourne **E**. The road climbs through woods and then crosses the bleak chalk uplands where Hardy imagined Tess slaving in the winter rains at a farm appropriately named 'Flintcombe Ash'.

Continue to the T-junction in Cheselbourne and then turn left, signposted Melcombe Bingham. When you reach a junction bear left for Melcombe and Ansty. The road runs through Melcombe Bingham to a T-junction at Ansty Cross. Turn right signposted Hilton and Milton Abbas. Pass a lane on the left and, when the road divides, take the left-hand road for Hilton. 'Hilton' is the Saxon term for 'hidden', and this tiny hamlet of grey flint and white-washed cottages with deep thatched roofs still seems far removed from the bustle of twentieth-century life. There is parking by the church which has many treasures including a set of fifteenth-century panel-paintings.

Follow the road through Hilton to Milton Abbey. Beautifully framed in a wooded hollow of the downs, the graceful twelfth- and fifteenth-century abbey church stands beside a huge eighteenth-century mansion. The church is open for visitors and the mansion, now a school, is open during the school holidays. **To visit the church continue past a lane on the right with a no-through-road sign. Turn right down the next lane on the right to the church car park.**

The tour continues down the wooded valley. Pass the lake and bear left sign-posted Winterborne Stickland to drive through Milton Abbas. The trim uniformity of this picture-postcard village, composed of a single street lined with rows of almost identical thatched cottages, is broken only by some brick and flint almshouses and the eighteenth-century church. When Joseph Damer, later Earl of Dorchester, bought the Milton Estates he pulled down the village clustered about the abbey and, in 1768, asked 'Capability' Brown to design a new Milton Abbas well out of sight of his windows.

• PLACES OF INTEREST •

Hambledon Hill

The eastern slopes of the hill are very steep and proved an ideal training ground for General Wolfe's troops before they scaled the heights of Abraham to capture Quebec. In 1645 the Dorset Clubmen, some 2,000 villagers desperate to put an end to the Civil War, rallied behind the embankments on the hilltop. They were routed by fifty of Cromwell's dragoons. Many were taken prisoner and locked up for the night in Shroton Church. Next morning they were allowed to return home having promised to cause no more disturbances.

Milton Abbey

A monastery was founded in this beautiful valley by King Athelstan in 938. The original wooden church was burnt to the ground in 1309 and the building of the present church began in 1331 and continued up to the Dissolution of the Monasteries in 1539. Although unfinished, the abbey is superb, it has a fine tower and beautiful windows. Inside there are many treasures including a delicately-carved altar-screen, a rood-loft with medieval portraits said to represent King Athelstan and his mother, and an oak hanging tabernacle, possibly the only one in England.

The abbey church is all that remains of the monastic buildings. At the Dissolution the property was given by Henry VIII to Sir John Tregonwell. In 1752 Joseph Damer bought the estates from the Tregonwell family. He demolished all the domestic buildings except the Abbot's Hall which was incorporated into the new mansion he had designed by Sir William Chambers and James Wyatt.

The abbey tearooms are open Easter, July and August.

After the village turn left at the T-junction signposted Winterborne Stickland. Pass the Farm Museum on the right. At the Y-junction take the right-hand road to approach Winterborne Stickland. Drive over the road signed for Houghton and then turn left signposted Turnworth and Blandford Forum. Just past the drive to Turnworth House there is a National Trust car park on the left. A beautiful short walk leads from the car park through woods to the remains of the prehistoric and Roman settlement of Ringmoor surrounded by over thirty acres of narrow Celtic fields.

The road now rises to a picnic site by the beacon on the top of Okeford Hill. Splendid walks with magnificent views can be taken from here – a leaflet with details is available from the Tourist Office in Blandford. Continue down-hill to a T-junction and turn right for Okeford Fitzpaine. In the centre of the village turn right and then right again for Shillingstone. The road meets the A357 opposite the school in Shillingstone. Turn right along the A357 to follow the west bank of the River Stour to Durweston. The road bears left to cross the river and meet the A350. Turn right signposted Blandford to the junction with the B3082. Turn right along the B3082 to return to the centre of Blandford Forum.

Milton Abbey now stands alone in its green bowl in the Dorset hills. The village that clustered around it was demolished in the eighteenth century

THE DORSET UPLANDS

60 MILES – 3 HOURS
START AND FINISH AT DORCHESTER

Sparkling chalk streams carve deep valleys through the downs north of Dorchester, and this tour explores three of the loveliest of these valleys as it runs beside the River Cerne. It takes you past Cerne Abbas, one of the most attractive of all Dorset villages, follows the River Frome to Cattistock and returns along the west bank of tiny Sydling Water, one of the county's hidden gems. Readers of the novels of Thomas Hardy will recognise the country of The Woodlanders *and enjoy the visit to Evershot, Hardy's 'Evershead'.*

Leave Dorchester's Top o'Town roundabout heading north along the A37 signposted Yeovil. The embankments which once supported the town walls are on your right. **Pass a joining road on the right to bear left over the River Frome. At the roundabout keep ahead signposted Yeovil and Sherborne. Take the next road on the right, the A352, signposted Cerne Abbas and Sherborne. Continue straight over the crossroads in Charminster.** The road runs north to Cerne Abbas along the valley of the River Cerne bordered by gently-rounded hills. On each side the smooth turf is broken by ridges and embankments, the remains of ancient villages and field systems.

After about 3 miles, as the road leaves Godmanstone, the thatched Smiths Arms inn is on the right. It is said to be the smallest public house in England.

The enchanting village of Cerne Abbas is about 2 miles further up the valley. Do not take the first road on the right signposted to the village, but continue for about ¼ mile and turn right into the parking space signed Viewpoint and Picnic Area at the top of the third road leading to the village **A**. From here you have a splendid

• PLACES OF INTEREST •

Cerne Abbas
This delightful village lies cradled in the downs looking, in the words of the Dorset historian Sir Frederick Treves, 'warm and comfortable, curled up like a dormouse in a sunny corner'.

The village grew up around the Benedictine abbey founded here in AD 987 by Aethelmar, Earl of Devon and Cornwall. The ruined gatehouse retains an exquisitely-carved oriel window. The ruins stand behind Abbey House at the head of Abbey Street.

The abbey's huge fourteenth-century tithe barn (part of which is now a farmhouse) can be seen from the Dorchester road, south of the village.

Overlooking Abbey Street is the Parish Church of St Mary. It dates mostly from the fifteenth century, although the beautiful chancel is thirteenth century and is decorated with medieval wall paintings. The fine east window glows with fifteenth-century glass believed to have been rescued from the abbey at the Dissolution. A homely touch is provided by the gargoyle with a gaping mouth projecting from the side of the south porch. This allowed the smoke to escape from a small hearth inside the porch where fires could be lit to warm those attending parish meetings.

Opposite the church jettied half-timbered cottages overhang worn flagstones.

The abbey ruins are open for visitors for a small entrance fee.

Cerne Abbas Giant
From the abbey ruins a path leads over the churchyard to the Cerne Abbas Giant. This mighty figure, over 180 feet (55 metres) high is still something of a mystery. It is believed he was carved during the Roman occupation, or possibly earlier by Stone Age tribes. It could be that his eminently virile figure was meant to represent the Emperor Commodus who declared himself the reincarnation of Hercules in AD 191, but many believe he was more native in origin, perhaps a Celtic fertility god.

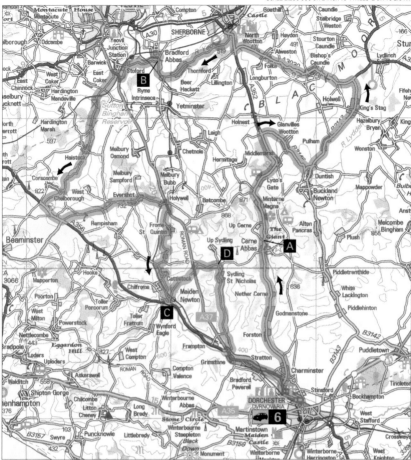

view of the famous Cerne Abbas giant, his white outline carved out of the turf on the hill immediately opposite, appropriately named Giant Hill.

Cerne Abbas is a small compact village best explored on foot, so drive down the road towards the village for only a few yards then turn left down a lane to a car park and picnic place on the left. Walk a little further down the lane to the stream. Do not cross, but turn right to follow the streamside. Continue over a bridge to Mill Lane which leads to the entrance to the abbey and the centre of the village.

Return to the A352 at A and turn right to continue up the valley past Minterne Parva to Minterne Magna. The entrance to Minterne Gardens, a woodland garden through which the River Cerne runs over a series of cascades forming small lakes, is on the right. The car park for the gardens is on the left, opposite the entrance.

The valley narrows as the road runs through Dogbury Gate between the crests of High Stoy and Little Minterne Hill. Now there is a dramatic change of scene. The downs curve away west and east and below, stretching to the horizon, lies the

The Cerne Abbas giant – his origin still puzzles historians

35

Beautiful woodland gardens surround Minterne House

Blackmoor Vale laced with tiny fields and dotted with small hills and woods. It was here, where the chalk hills give way to the clay soils of the vale, that Thomas Hardy set the second edition of *The Woodlanders*.

Follow the A352 into the vale following the signs for Sherborne. Some remnants of the great forests that once covered the vale are passed as the road runs through Middlemarsh. **Continue past Middlemarsh Common and turn right along the B3146 signposted Buckland Newton and Glanvilles Wootton.** The church in Glanvilles Wootton,

set in a hollow in the downs and approached through an avenue of flowering trees, has a fascinating chantry chapel. **At the T-junction in Glanvilles Wootton turn right.**

To see the church, ignore the first lane on the left, Rectory Lane, but turn left down the next lane past Church Farm.

Retrace the route to the B3146 and turn left to climb the side of Dungeon Hill. Keep to the main road at a junction, bearing left for Mappowder and Pulham. At a T-junction turn left along the B3143 signposted

Sturminster Newton and Pulham. **Drive through Pulham towards the village of King's Stag.** The village takes its name from a romantic story told by the county historian Hutchins. While out hunting, King Henry III spared the life of 'a beautiful and goodly white hart'. When the King later heard the stag had been killed by Sir Thomas de la Lynde he laid heavy fines on this part of the Blackmoor Vale which is often known as the Vale of the White Hart. The hart died close to a bridge over the River Lydden and the village of King's Stag received its present name.

Drive through King's Stag to meet the A3030. Turn left signposted Bishop's Caundle to cross the Caundle brook. There are enchanting views over the lush woods and hills of the vale as you drive through Bishop's Caundle. **Keep to the A3030 as it runs through Alweston to meet the A352. Turn right for Sherborne, then take the road on the left signposted Thornford. At the T-junction turn left for Thornford down the valley of the River Yeo. Drive through the village, pass a joining road on the left, and keep to the same road as it heads north for Bradford Abbas.**

The route turns left B just before Bradford Abbas, but it is worth making a short detour to explore this charming village. Houses built of golden Ham stone cluster around a church dating from the twelfth century with a magnificent fifteenth-century west tower.

To see the church keep ahead, cross the River Yeo into the village and then take the first turning on the left to the church. There is room to park here.

To continue the tour retrace the route over the River Yeo to B and turn right signposted Clifton Maybank and Stoford. At the

---

• *PLACES OF INTEREST* •

Minterne Gardens
A particularly lovely woodland garden, especially in the spring when the rhododendrons and azaleas are at their best. Open 1 April–31 October, daily, 10–7.

Bradford Abbas
Until the Dissolution the manor and the church were owned by the Abbots of Sherborne which accounts for the second part of the village name. The parish church of St Mary the Virgin is one of the finest in Dorset, famous for its tower and richly-decorated west front. Inside there is much to admire, including a beautifully-

carved hexagonal Jacobean pulpit, a superb fifteenth-century font and a stone rood-screen of the same date. Many of the bench ends are delicately carved. A medieval oak chest, of the dug out type with ancient locks and grooves for partitions, stands in the north aisle.

Not far from the church is the Rose and Crown pub, dating from the late fifteenth century. It has a splendid stone fireplace surrounded by panelling. Possibly built as a rest house for the monks, it was later used as a malt-house.

T-junction in Stoford turn left signposted Melbury and Dorchester. The road runs south then turns right to meet the A37. Turn right to cross the railway then take the first road on the left signposted Sutton Bingham. The road runs under the railway then crosses a branch of the T-shaped Sutton Bingham Reservoir. After crossing there is a car park and picnic place immediately on the left. Tables under trees overlook the reservoir colourful with small boats. The reservoir was constructed in 1956 and has become a haven for wild birds – over 146 species have been recorded.

Rolling chalk downlands rise ahead as the road runs beside the reservoir to Halstock. **Keep straight on through Halstock signposted Corscombe. Drive through Corscombe, past the Fox pub and the lane to the church, to meet the A356. Turn left and, after about a mile, take the road on the left signposted Evershot. Drive through Benville following the Evershot signs. Keep straight on through Evershot to pass the church** where the poet Crabbe was once vicar. Just past here is 'Tess Cottage'. In his novel *Tess of the d'Urbervilles* Hardy allows Tess to breakfast at the cottage on

The remote and peaceful village of Sydling St Nicholas

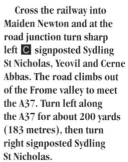

her long walk from Flintcombe Ash to Beaminster.

The road bears right at the end of the village to meet the A37. Turn right signposted Dorchester and continue for about ¼ mile. Take the first road on the right signposted Frome St Quintin and Chantmarle. Keep to this beautiful road as it winds down the Frome valley through Frome St Quintin. Turn right at a T-junction following the signs for Cattistock. At the next T-junction turn left to drive into Cattistock. Keep to the main road as it bears left then right through the village and continue down the valley following the signs for Maiden Newton.

Cross the railway into Maiden Newton and at the road junction turn sharp left ⒞ signposted Sydling St Nicholas, Yeovil and Cerne Abbas. The road climbs out of the Frome valley to meet the A37. Turn left along the A37 for about 200 yards (183 metres), then turn right signposted Sydling St Nicholas.

The road drops to a crossroads ⒟. Turn left to drive into the delightful village of Sydling St Nicholas hidden in the valley of Sydling Water. Pause here if you have time. The village is mainly composed of thatched yellow stone and flint cottages linked to each other by tiny bridges over Sydling Water. The Georgian manor incorporates part of a Tudor house owned by Sir Francis Walsingham in 1590. Beside it stands a tithe barn and close by is the shaft and pedestal of a medieval wayside cross. The village has the whole 5 miles of the Sydling Water valley to itself.

Follow the road by the stream past the watercress beds to meet the A37. Turn left for Dorchester. Keep ahead at the roundabout signed for Dorchester to drive up to Top o'Town roundabout. ▪

Evershot village, Thomas Hardy's 'Evershead'

STURMINSTER NEWTON, SHAFTESBURY AND GILLINGHAM

50 MILES – 3 HOURS
START AND FINISH AT STURMINSTER NEWTON

The small market towns close to the north Dorset border are visited on this tour including Shaftesbury, built on the site of an Iron Age hill-fort in a commanding position overlooking the Blackmoor Vale. The route runs through the leafy undulating countryside of the vale giving panoramic views past picturesque villages. One of these is Marnhull, immortalised by Thomas Hardy as 'Marlott' the home of his heroine in Tess of the d'Urbervilles. *And a visit to Fiddleford Manor is a 'must'!*

The wonderful timbered roof of Fiddleford Manor

From the market-place in Sturminster Newton head south along the B3092. **Cross the River Stour over the town's medieval bridge to meet the A357. Turn left signposted Shillingstone and Blandford along the wooded valley of the River Stour. In just over a mile turn left for Fiddleford Manor. Turn left into the car park.** A footpath leads to the manor set among green lawns beside the river. Restored by English Heritage and now open to the public the manor is one of the finest medieval buildings in Dorset. The roof of the great hall and the solar are splendidly timbered.

Turn left out of the car park and follow the lane past the entrance to Fiddleford Mill. The lane curves right to rejoin the A357. Turn left and, after 1/2 mile, turn left again signposted Hammoon. The village is named after the de Mohuns, a Norman family who held the land in the Middle Ages. **Continue over the crossroads signposted Manston and Child Okeford. Cross the bridge over the River Stour to a T-junction. Turn right signposted Child Okeford. Continue into Child Okeford village and, shortly after the village hall, take the road on the left signposted Shaftesbury. Keep straight on over the crossroads to meet the A350. Turn left signposted Shaftesbury.** Eastwards rise the graceful outlines of the north Dorset downs.

At the crossroads in Sutton Waldron you may like to make a short detour to see a most unusual church. If so, turn left following the sign for the village centre. Turn left again up Church Road where there is room to park. The church, richly adorned by Owen Jones, has been described by John Betjeman as 'one of the best and most lovely examples of Victorian architecture'. **Return to the A350 and turn left to continue north through Fontmell Magna and Compton Abbas.** North of Compton Abbas Melbury

A magnificent medieval bridge spans the River Stour at the approaches to Sturminster Newton

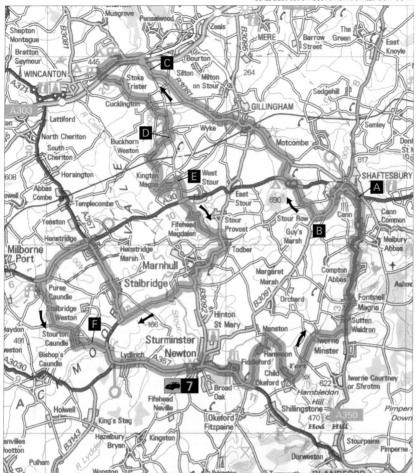

Hill rises to a height of 863 feet (263 metres), its sides deeply scored by medieval strip lynchets.

The A350 dips to cross a stream beside a mill then approaches Shaftesbury. At the roundabout turn left following the sign for the town centre A . The road runs through the town to a junction. Bear left here and keep to the same road as it curves right. After a few yards turn left along the B3091 following the sign for Sturminster Newton.

A turning on the left is signed for the Abbey ruins. Take this if you wish to explore the ruins and enjoy magnificent views over the Vale of Blackmoor. Return to the B3091 and turn left.

• PLACES OF INTEREST •

Sturminster Newton

This small market town stands on a rise overlooking the River Stour. Its old streets are a fascinating blend of medieval gables, coaching inns and pretty Georgian cottages. Outside the thatched market-house in the centre of the Market Square are the octagonal stone steps of a cross. This was the site of Sturminster's famous livestock market, now moved to the north of the town.

The Church of St Mary was rebuilt in the nineteenth century, but has a lovely fifteenth-century wagon roof decorated with carved wooden angels.

Another interesting building is the old Boys School, built on a massive scale with heavy gables and mullioned windows.

The charm of Sturminster captivated Thomas Hardy and his wife Emma. They rented Riverside Villa where they spent their happiest time together. To see the house follow Rickett's Lane from the Market Place, follow the path over the recreation ground and then turn left through the gate at the far side. Riverside Villa is on the corner with a splendid view west across the River Stour to the Blackmoor Vale.

Sturminster Mill is open Easter–end September, Saturday, Sunday, Monday and Thursday, 11–5. Telephone: Sturminster Newton (01258) 473760

39

The road drops steeply down St Johns Hill. **Pass a road on the right signposted Todber and continue to a T-junction. Keep to the main road as it turns right past a church. In a mile turn right signposted Motcombe and Gillingham ** **B** **. At the T-junction turn left and continue on this road signposted Motcombe and Gillingham to meet the A30. Turn left signposted Sherborne. Continue for about ½ mile and then turn right signposted Motcombe**

and Gillingham to meet the B3081. Turn left for Gillingham. In the Middle Ages Gillingham manor was part of a Royal Hunting Forest, and the route passes the remains of a hunting lodge built by King John in 1199, now known as King's Court Palace.

To see the site of the palace drive through Ham and, as you approach Gillingham, you will see a sign for the Dorset Rare Breeds Centre on the right. About ½ mile after this, turn right down Kingscourt

Road and park near the entrance to the site.

Return to the B3081 and turn right to Gillingham. Cross the River Lodden, the railway and the River Stour to a roundabout. Bear left along the B3081 signposted Mere and Bourton. Go straight ahead at the traffic lights and at the next junction turn left, still on the B3081, signposted Wincanton.

After about 3½ miles, when you see the A303 ahead, turn left following the sign for Bourton, Charlton Musgrove, Stoke Trister, Zeals and Mere **C**. The road runs under the A303 to a T-junction. Turn left and continue for about 1½ miles. Turn left signposted Stoke Trister. The road runs back under the A303 past Stoke Trister Church into a valley then climbs a steep ridge of downland towards Cucklington. **Just before you reach the top turn sharp left up the little lane leading to the church where there is room to park.** The church has a small chapel dedicated to St Barbara, the Patron Saint of Hills. This is highly appropriate as there is a breathtaking view westwards from the churchyard. Footpaths lead from the church along the top of the hill.

To continue the tour turn left from the lane to the church uphill to a T-junction. Bear right when the road divides and keep straight on along the main road (left-hand road). Keep ahead signposted Buckhorn Weston. The road follows the crest of the ridge with views all the way and then curves east.

At a T-junction turn right to continue over the next crossroads (Quarr Cross). Continue for ¼ mile to take the next turn on the right downhill towards Buckhorn Weston **D**. At the T-junction turn left to drive through the village. The road

---

• PLACES OF INTEREST •

Shaftesbury
Shaftesbury is one of the oldest towns in England. It stands at over 700 feet (213 metres) on a promontory overlooking the Blackmoor Vale. It was fortified in the ninth century by King Alfred who also founded an abbey here for his daughter who became its first abbess. In AD 981 King Edward the Martyr was buried here and the town prospered as a place of pilgrimage. At the Dissolution the abbey was destroyed, but the outlines of the great church can still be traced.

Explore the town on foot if you can to enjoy the magnificent views, especially from Castle Hill, where you can see as far as Glastonbury Tor and the steep,

cobbled Gold Hill, lined on one side with eighteenth-century cottages and on the other by the ancient buttressed abbey walls.
Interesting buildings include the Grosvenor Hotel, a coaching inn which houses the Chevy Chase

sideboard carved from a single piece of oak.
Shaftesbury Abbey and Museum, Park Walk. These are the ruins of the Benedictine abbey church. The museum contains many excavated artifacts. Open Easter–September, daily, 10–5.30. Telephone: Shaftesbury (01747) 852910
Shaftesbury Local History Museum, Gold Hill. Tells the story of Shaftesbury. Open Easter–September, daily, 11–5. Telephone: (01747) 852157

Gillingham
Gillingham is a pleasant market town situated to the north of the Blackmoor Vale on the borders of Somerset and Wiltshire. The town has a long history and the name 'Gillingham' is Saxon in origin. Several fine seventeenth- and eighteenth-century houses grace the town. In the 1820's John Constable painted the picturesque bridge over Shreen Water. This painting 'Old Gillingham Bridge' hangs in the Tate Gallery.
Today the town is an important business and shopping centre

Purse Caundle Manor
A beautiful Elizabethan manor house with an exquisite miniature oriel window overlooking the street through the village. Now a much-loved family home.
Open May–September, Thursday and Sunday, 2–5. Also Bank Holiday Monday.

passes the church and a joining road on the right, runs under a railway bridge and over the Filley Brook and, after 1¼ miles, comes to a T-junction. **Turn left signposted Gillingham to enter Kington Magna. At the T-junction in the village turn left and, after a few yards, turn left again.** The lane curves right to run uphill past Kington Magna Church.

Continue to a crossroads E where you turn right signposted Marnhull. Keep ahead over the A30 signposted Fifehead Magdalen. When the main road turns sharply right turn left, signposted Todber and Stour Provost, to drive through Fifehead Magdalen. The road curves right to cross the River Stour and meet the B3092. Turn right signposted Sturminster Newton. Keep to the B3092 as it turns right for Marnhull and drive up to the church. There are medieval wall paintings here and an east window designed by William Morris. Nearby is Nash Court, once the home of Henry VIII's sixth wife, Catherine Parr. But perhaps the village is best known as 'Marlott', the home of Thomas

Hardy's heroine Tess, in his novel *Tess of the d'Urbervilles.*

Follow the main road as it curves left by the church. Pass a lane on the left and then turn right signposted Stalbridge. After about 4 miles, when you meet the A357, turn right signposted Templecombe to drive through Stalbridge, a pleasant market town. On the right you pass the finest market cross in Dorset. Built of golden stone it is 30 feet (9 metres) high, sculptured, and dates from the fourteenth century. **Continue along the A357.** On the left is the long wall of Stalbridge Park which once surrounded a seventeenth-century house, the home of the scientist Robert Boyle. The house was burned down in 1820.

Drive through Henstridge and, when you meet the A30, turn left signposted Sherborne. Continue for 2½ miles and then turn left signposted Purse Caundle. Fifteenth-century Purse Caundle manor is on the right. This attractive manor, its stones mellowed by age to a soft dove grey, is a family home, and you can be shown round by the owner. The ghosts of

King John's hounds are said to haunt the grounds.

Keep straight on past the church for Stourton Caundle. At the crossroads turn right to drive into the village. Drive past the pub and keep to the main road as it bears left signposted Lydlinch and Sturminster Newton. After ¾ mile, at the T-junction F, turn right signposted Lydlinch and Sturminster Newton. Keep on to meet the A357 then turn right signposted Sturminster Newton.

The road runs through Lydlinch and a road on the right leads to the church. The bells of Lydlinch Church chiming across the meadows inspired William Barnes, the great Dorset poet, to write one of his finest poems. Barnes was born at Rushay, a farm in the nearby parish of Bagber.

Continue along the A357 towards Sturminster Newton. On the left a lane leads down to Sturminster Mill. This has been renovated and is now in working order. The mill is open to the public and stone-ground flour can be purchased. **Turn left along the B3092 to cross the bridge and return to the centre of Sturminster Newton.** ◼

SHERBORNE, CADBURY CASTLE AND THE MELBURYS

45 MILES – 3 HOURS
START AND FINISH AT SHERBORNE

There is a definite air of mystery and romance about this tour in the north-west corner of Dorset. From Sherborne, with its two castles once owned by Sir Walter Raleigh, the route runs north to Cadbury hill-fort, possibly the site of King Arthur's Camelot. The route then turns south to give magnificent views from the crests of some of Dorset's highest hills before returning to Sherborne through a succession of old-world villages with evocative names such as Hermitage and Melbury Bubb.

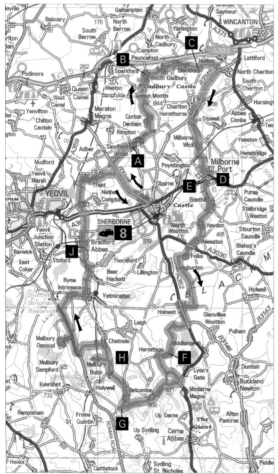

SCALE 1:250 000 OR 1 INCH TO 4 MILES *1 CM TO 2.5 KM*

Leave Sherborne heading north along the B3148 signposted Marston Magna. After 2¹/₂ miles turn right signposted Sandford Orcas. At the T-junction turn right to meet another T-junction in Sandford Orcas village. **Turn left A to the church and manor house, both on the right.** The Elizabethan manor surrounded by attractive gardens is open to the public.

From the manor turn left to retrace the route down the lane to **A**. Keep straight on signposted Sherborne. After a few yards turn left signposted Holway, Corton Denham and Poyntington. At the Y-junction take the left-hand road signposted Corton Denham. Ignore a joining road on the left and, when the road divides, take the left-hand road signposted Corton Denham. High downland ridges rise either side of the road as it heads north to this ancient village almost enclosed by hills. The houses follow the spring line of Corton Hill. Along the top of Corton ridge, west of the village, runs a pre-Roman track which possibly once connected the great hill-fort of Maiden Castle near

Dorchester with Cadbury hill-fort 2 miles to the north.

Drive through Corton Denham and climb Corton Hill. Bear right when the road divides signposted South Cadbury. Ahead rise the steep slopes of Cadbury hill-fort. **Turn right at the T-junction signposted South Cadbury. Bear left towards the village at the foot of the hill.**

The sign on the left of the road indicating a car park on the right is partly obscured by trees, so look carefully for the car park entrance about 50 yards (46 metres) before the South Cadbury village sign. If you miss it drive a little further down the road where there is room to park on the left by the wall of the churchyard. A short, but rather steep, footpath leads from Castle Lane, close to the South Cadbury village sign, to the top of the fort. Apart from the fort's historical interest and associations with King Arthur, it is worth the climb to enjoy a breathtaking view far over the Somerset levels to Glastonbury.

To continue the tour drive past the church on your left

Sandford Orcas manor house claims to have thirty-five ghosts!

and, almost immediately, you come to a crossroads. **Turn right signposted Compton Pauncefoot** ∎ . At the T-junction, as you enter the village, turn left and then right at the next T-junction. The road now divides. **Keep to the main road which bears left round the northern boundary of Compton Park. Drive over the crossroads signposted Blackford and Maperton.** Continue over the crossroads in Blackford village and keep on for Maperton.

Bear right in Maperton, uphill, ∎ **past the church signposted North Cheriton**

and Sherborne. After ³/₄ mile bear right signposted Sherborne to meet the B3145. **Turn right along the B3145 and keep to this road as it runs south to Charlton Horethorne.** Follow the main road through the village for Milborne Wick and Sherborne as far as a junction. **Leave the B3145 and take the left-hand road signposted Milborne Port. Continue for about a mile then turn right signposted Milborne Wick.**

Bear a little left over the crossroads in the centre of the village to continue south under the railway for

---

• PLACES OF INTEREST •

Sherborne
Sherborne is a town of great charm and character. Built of golden stone, it stands on the north bank of the River Yeo surrounded by wooded countryside. The town was a cathedral city in Saxon times with St Aldhelm as its first bishop. A Benedictine monastery was established in the ninth century, the monks taking over the cathedral as their abbey church. Rebuilt in the fifteenth century, the beautiful abbey retains evidence of Saxon and Norman work, but its chief glory is the intricately-carved fan vaulting above the nave and choir.

The main street, Cheap Street, is a pleasing mix of medieval,

Georgian and Victorian buildings. The Conduit at the southern end was originally the monks' wash place. It was moved to its present site to act as a market-house after the Dissolution.

In 1550 the Sherborne School for boys was founded taking over many of the former monastic buildings, including the Abbot's Hall which became the chapel. Education is important in Sherborne. The town has other major boys' and girls' public schools and also several private and state schools.

East of the town are Sherborne's two castles, known locally as the Old and the New. The Old castle dates from the twelfth century. It was slighted

by Cromwell in the Civil War. In 1592 Sir Walter Raleigh rented the ruins intending to rebuild them, but in 1594 he decided to build another castle in the grounds instead. It was here that a servant doused him with beer while he was smoking tobacco, believing him to be on fire! Since 1617 additions have been made to the castle by the Digby family who, in the eighteenth century, commissioned 'Capability' Brown to design the grounds.

Sherborne Castle is open Easter Saturday–end September, Thursday, Saturday, Sunday and Bank Holiday Mondays, 1.30–5. Grounds and tearoom open from 12.30. Telephone: Sherborne (01935) 813182

Upside-down Saxon carvings decorate the font at Melbury Bubb

Milborne Port. Keep ahead through Milborne Port and bear right at the T-junction in the town centre **D** to meet the A30. Turn right for a few yards along the A30 signposted Sherborne. Pass a joining road on the right, then turn left down Goathill Road **E**. The road dips to cross a stream at Goathill then runs through the beautiful oak and beech woods clothing Hanover Hill. When the road divides take the right-hand road signposted Haydon and Alweston. At the top of the hill you will see the iron gates of Sherborne Park on the right. You can leave the car here and take a delightful walk following the yellow arrow footpath sign through the gates.

Continue the tour through Haydon and Alweston to meet the A3030. Drive straight across to follow the lane to

Folke. At the T-junction in Folke turn right. The road curves left to head south towards the north Dorset downs.

Continue for about 3 miles through attractive country-side to a T-junction. Turn right to meet the A352 and then left along the A352 signposted Dorchester for about a mile. Now turn right signposted Hermitage past the lodge at the gates of Holnest Park. Drive into Hermitage and keep to the main road as it turns right at the T-junction in the village. Turn left at the next T-junction **F** following a dark wooden sign to the church where there is room to park. The village is named after the hermitage that was once built here by Augustinian monks. Now sheep nibble the grass in the tiny churchyard beside a green overlooked by a sixteenth-century farmhouse.

Return to **F** and continue to a T-junction. Turn left signposted Minterne Magna and Cerne Abbas. The road climbs the lower slopes of High Stoy. The road descends through woodlands to meet the A352 at Dogbury Gate. Turn right along the A352 signposted Dorchester. After a few hundred yards take the next road on the right signposted Batcombe and Evershot. The road climbs through woods and then turns left along the crest of a high

downland ridge. Stop in Batcombe car park and picnic place on the right to enjoy the view. Northwards lies the Blackmoor Vale and to the west the horizon is fringed by the Mendip Hills. Looking south, streams carve steep valleys through the chalk as they run to meet the River Frome north of Dorchester.

Turn right from the car park to continue along the ridge. About 30 yards (27 metres) after a turning on the right for the Friary, look carefully on the right-hand verge of the road for a small stone pillar about $3^{1}/_{2}$ feet (1.1 metres) high. This is the Cross-in-Hand, the subject of legend and superstition (see places of interest box). About a mile further be ready to take an unsignposted road on the right **G**. A very steep descent leads down to Batcombe, almost hidden in a hollow of the hill.

From Batcombe the road runs to a T-junction. Bear left for Chetnole. Turn right at the next junction signposted Melbury Bubb. At the next junction turn left for Melbury Bubb and, after a few yards, left again **H** to drive into this tiny village. Park by the church. It is possible that Thomas Hardy had this village in mind when he described Little Hintock, in the first edition of *The Woodlanders*, as being 'snipped out of the hillside'. The church is lit by brass oil lamps and has a beaker-shaped Saxon font with upside-down carvings of a dragon and hounds chasing a deer.

Return to **H**, turn left signposted Chetnole, and keep ahead beside the Wriggle River. Turn left as you enter the village, signposted Dorchester and Yeovil. The road bears right to meet the A37. Turn right signed for Yeovil. After a mile turn left for Melbury Osmond. At the T-junction turn left and follow the road as it bears left to the

The view over the Somerset Levels from Cadbury Castle

church where there is room to park. Charming stone cottages surrounded by colourful gardens cluster either side of a lane leading down to a watersplash. Thomas Hardy's parents were married in the church. The cottage where Jemima, Hardy's mother, lived as a girl is close by.

Return to the A37 and turn left for Yeovil. After 2 miles turn right for Ryme Intrinseca. Follow the road left at the T-junction for Ryme and then right for Yetminster past the church. At the T-junction in Yetminster turn left signposted Thornford and Sherborne. Keep to the main road as it runs north to cross the railway to a T-junction. Turn left signposted Bradford Abbas. Cross the River Yeo to enter this beautiful Ham stone village. Take the first road on the left to a parking area in front of the church. This fifteenth-century church is famous for its elegant tower and richly-carved west front.

With the church on your left retrace the route for about 30 yards (27 metres) and then turn left along Back Lane . Keep ahead over the crossroads signposted Over Compton to meet the A30. Drive straight across and follow the lane ahead. After the lane bears right for a few yards turn left signposted Trent. At the Y-junction bear right into the village to park in the lane by the church and manor. The church has an old rood-screen, and rusted helmets and gauntlets hang over the effigies in the manorial chapel. After his defeat at the battle of Worcester, Charles II was hidden by Colonel Wyndham for a fortnight in the manor house.

Turn right just past the church, signposted Sherborne. Keep to the main road following the Sherborne signs to meet the B3148. Turn right to drive 2 miles to Sherborne.

• PLACES OF INTEREST •

Sandford Orcas

This charming house has survived practically unaltered through the centuries. It was built in the 1550s by Edward Noyle, then aged twenty-one, who later became Sheriff of Somerset and Dorset. It is reputedly the most haunted house in Britain, with no less than thirty-five ghostly residents!

Open Easter Monday 10–6. May–September, Sunday, 2–6 and Monday 10–6. Telephone: Corton Denham (01963) 220206

Cadbury Castle (hill-fort)

This magnificent hill-fort, covering eighteen acres, is the focal point of many ancient trackways. It is encircled by four huge banks with a height of over 40 feet (12 metres) in places.

The fort shows evidence of settlement from around 3000 BC to the eleventh century. During the Iron Age a small town developed within the fortifications which became the capital of the Durotriges. It became important as a centre of trade and culture and the focus of a religious cult. Around AD 500 massive refortification took place with the building of timber and dry-stone walling defences.

The foundations of a cruciform church and a large timber hall have been excavated and it is possible this was the fortress of a powerful Christian leader such as King Arthur. Cadbury became associated with the Camelot of Arthurian romance in the sixteenth century, and it is tempting to picture Arthur here planning his great victory over the Saxons at *Mons Badonis*.

At the beginning of the eleventh century coins were minted at Cadbury, but the site declined in importance after the mint was moved to Ilchester.

Cross-in-Hand, near Batcombe

In Hardy's novel *Tess of the d'Urbervilles* Tess is forced by her seducer Alec to place her hand on the cross and swear she will never tempt him with her beauty again. An old shepherd tells her it is a 'thing of ill-omen'. But in one of his poems Hardy tells a charming story about the stone. A priest from Cerne Abbey was summoned one very stormy night to take Holy Communion to a dying man in the Blackmoor Vale. On the way he dropped the pyx containing the blessed bread. He hurried back to find it and saw a light shining on the hill. The light fell on the pyx, and surrounding it was an adoring circle of animals. The priest was just in time to give the last sacraments to the dying man. In gratitude the priest had the stone placed on the spot where the pyx had lain.

Sherborne Castle built by Sir Walter Raleigh in 1594

BEAMINSTER AND THE MARSHWOOD VALE

50 MILES – 3 HOURS
START AND FINISH AT BEAMINSTER

The visit to Forde Abbey, originally a Cistercian monastery but now a stately home surrounded by beautiful gardens, must be the highlight of this tour in west Dorset. From Beaminster the route runs through attractive villages sheltered by the highest hills in the county. Short walks to the summits of Pilsdon Pen and Lambert's Castle Hill are rewarded by splendid views. The tour returns over the Marshwood Vale and along the picturesque valley of the River Hooke.

Leave Beaminster heading south along the A3066 signposted Netherbury and Bridport. After ³/₄ mile the entrance to Parnham House is on the right. Turn right here if you wish to visit **Parnham.** This is a Tudor mansion, now the home of John and Jenny Makepeace. John Makepeace furniture is designed and manufactured in the house. **About ¼ mile past the**

entrance to Parnham turn right signposted Netherbury, beside the River Brit. Continue ahead past a turning on the right and keep to the main road as it bears right signposted Bowood and Broadwindsor. At the T-junction keep to the main road as it bears right, again signposted Bowood and Broadwindsor. Cross the River Brit and carry on

through the attractive village of Netherbury.
   At the top of the hill bear right signposted Broad-windsor and drive past the church. Keep to the main road as it turns left and continue to meet the B3162. Turn right signposted Broadwindsor, Crewkerne and Chard. The tree-clad slopes of Lewesdon Hill rise ahead. **After a little more than a mile**

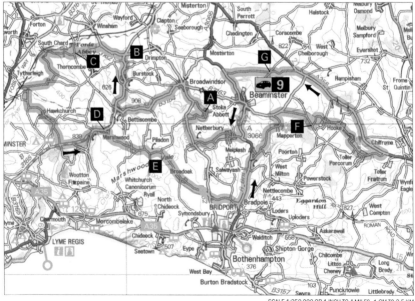

SCALE 1:250 000 OR 1 INCH TO 4 MILES 1 CM TO 2.5 KM

turn right at the crossroads signposted Stoke Abbot. The lane tunnels beneath trees and then turns left to enter this enchanting village. Golden stone thatched houses, ringed with bright gardens are tucked in the dips and hollows at the foot of Lewesdon Hill.

Careful navigation is needed here! Just past a sign on the left pointing to the village hall take the next road on the left, uphill . The sign to Broadwindsor is not visible before you turn. To explore the village on foot park beside the road just past the turning.

From Stoke Abbot the road climbs to run through a gap between Lewesdon and Waddon hills. On the northern slopes of Waddon Hill, on the right, there is the outline of a large Roman fort, strategically placed to command the approaches to Somerset. The most interesting find during

Golden stone cottages at Stoke Abbot

excavations in the 1880s was a first century AD scabbard made of iron with gold alloy.

As you near the top of the hill take care as the road rises abruptly to meet the B3162. Bear right for Broadwindsor. At the junction with the B3163 in Broadwindsor bear left signposted Drimpton and Chard. The road curves left to a junction. Turn left along the

B3164 signposted Axminster and Lyme Regis. The old George Inn is on your right as you turn. A plaque states that the fugitive Charles II spent a night here in 1651 after his defeat at the battle of Worcester. He was acting the part of groom to Juliana Coningsby on his flight from Charmouth to the manor at Trent.

Continue along the B3164 towards the smooth green slopes of Pilsdon Pen. At 908 feet (277 metres) it is Dorset's highest hill. After about 2 miles there is a layby on the left. Stop here for a magnificent view south over the great bowl of the Marshwood Vale. If you cross the road and take the footpath to the top of Pilsdon Pen the view is even more breathtaking!

Continue along the B3164 to Birdsmoorgate. Turn right

• PLACES OF INTEREST •

Beaminster
Set in an amphitheatre of green hills beside the River Brit, Beaminster is one of the most appealing small towns in the south-west. There is a special timeless quality about its quiet streets and central square surrounded by early nineteenth-century houses built of golden Ham Hill stone.

The comparatively modern appearance of the town is due to several disastrous fires. The worst occurred in 1644 when almost all the town was burnt. Royalist troops were billeted in the town at the time and, during an argument between French and Cornish contingents, a musket was discharged into a thatched roof. There were other fires in 1684 and 1781, but the town prospered as a market and centre for the woollen cloth trade.

Fortunately, the fires spared Beaminster's magnificent church tower. It dates from the early

sixteenth century and is richly decorated and pinnacled. The interior was mainly restored in the nineteenth century and contains an imposing monument to George Strode and his wife who lived at nearby Parnham House.

Horn Park Gardens Here can be found rare plants, a woodland garden and a wild flower meadow. Unusual plants for sale. Open April–October 31, Tuesday, Wednesday, Sunday and Bank Holidays, 2–6. Telephone: (01308) 862212

Parnham House, near Beaminster
Parnham is a splendidly restored manor house with extensive gardens. Visitors can play croquet and picnic in the grounds. Refreshments and craft shop.
Open April–October, Wednesday, Sunday and Bank Holidays, 10–5. Telephone: Beaminster (01308) 862204

The view from Pilsdon Pen over the Marshwood Vale

Swans glide gracefully on the placid waters of the River Axe as it flows past Forde Abbey

along the B3165 signposted Blackdown and Crewkerne. After ¹/₂ mile you pass some iron gates on the left. Beyond them you will see Racedown House. William and Dorothy Wordsworth made their first home together at Racedown, arriving in September 1795 and staying until June 1797. Here, encouraged by Dorothy, Wordsworth recovered his belief in himself as a poet and rediscovered his delight in nature. Poems written at Racedown include *Lines left upon a Seat in a Yew-tree* and *The Ruined Cottage*.

Keep to the B3165 through Blackdown to Kittwhistle. Continue along the B3165 to the crossroads. Turn left **B** along the B3162 for Winsham and Chard. In just over a mile

turn left at Maudlin Cross signposted Axminster, Chard Junction and Forde Abbey. After about a mile follow the road round a right turn and, when the road turns left **C**, keep straight ahead following the sign downhill for Forde Abbey. The entrance to the house and garden is on the right.

After visiting the abbey return up the lane to **C**. Turn right signposted Chard Road and Axminster. The road runs down into the valley of the River Axe, the border with Somerset, to Chard Junction. At the T-junction turn left signposted Holditch and Hawkchurch. Shortly after this turn left again signposted for Holditch. After a mile turn right signposted Holditch. At the T-junction in the village

bear right to run past the entrance to Holditch Court. In a little over a mile turn left signposted Hawkchurch and Axminster to cross the River Blackwater and run south towards Castle. Keep to the main road as it bears left at a division, then left again at a T-junction signposted Hawkchurch. Follow the signs for Hawkchurch along a twisting road and drive through the village. Continue straight over the crossroads to meet the B3165. Turn left signposted Marshwood and Crewkerne. The road rises to run along a high ridge following the contours of Lambert's Castle Hill. A National Trust car park on the right gives access to a footpath leading to the top of the hill which is encircled by Iron Age earthworks. The entrance to the car park is difficult to spot from the road.

Pass a turning to Fishpond and, just after a sharp bends sign, look for a white gravel track on the right. Turn right along the track to the car park. A short walk will be rewarded with one of the finest views in Dorset. Looking south far over the Marshwood Vale and the coastal hills you can see Portland and the Fleet sheltered by Chesil beach. To the north and east are the Somerset and Wiltshire hills.

Return to the road, turn right and continue for Marshwood village, high on the northern ridge of the vale. Shortly after passing a little sixteenth-century thatched pub, the Bottle, leave the B3165 and turn right past the church signposted Broadoak and Mutton Street **D**. The road drops steeply downhill then runs more gently over the Marshwood Vale. Once, as its name suggests, the Marshwood Vale was a harsh and boggy wilderness, now it is pleasant undulating country watered by many streams and dotted with splendid oak trees.

Continue over a crossroads towards Shave Cross to a T-junction **E**. Turn right signposted Bridport. Opposite the pub in Shave Cross bear left signposted Bridport, Stoke Abbott and Beaminster. Drive on through Broadoak to climb the western edge of the vale and meet the B3162 at Dottery. Cross straight over the B3162 signposted Pymore. The road dips and climbs before crossing the River Brit to meet the A3066. **Turn left along the A3066 signposted Beaminster. After 2½ miles pass the church at Melplash on the left and turn right opposite the pub signposted Hincknowle and Mapperton.** The road weaves through the hills and, after 2 miles, you will see the entrance to Mapperton Gardens on the right. The gardens surrounding the Tudor house are open to the public. The nearby village was deserted after the population suffered from the plague of 1660.

The road curves left to meet the B3163. Turn right signposted Maiden Newton and Dorchester. After ½ mile turn right signposted Hooke. The road runs over the downs and through woodland for about 1½ miles. Turn left **F** signposted Hooke and Kingcombe into the secluded valley of the River Hooke.

• PLACES OF INTEREST •

Forde Abbey
Forde Abbey is an astonishing building. An elegant sixteenth- and seventeenth-century house is built around a Cistercian monastery. Although the abbey church has gone, together with the guest wing and three sides of the cloisters, the monks would recognise their dormitories, kitchen, refectories and chapter house.

The site by the River Axe was offered to the Cistercian monks in 1142 and became famous as a centre of learning. After the Dissolution the buildings were neglected for over a hundred years. In the seventeenth century Edmund Prideaux bought the abbey and transformed it into a 'palazzo' in the Italian style, combining new forms of English Baroque with some Gothic features. Outstanding among many beautiful rooms is the Upper Refectory with its fine timbered roof and carved panelling.

The Mortlake tapestries represent scenes from the Acts of the Apostles, painted by Raphael for the Sistine Chapel in Rome, and copied from the artist's original cartoons.

The house is the home of the Roper family who farm as the monks did, their main interests being a forest tree nursery, fruit growing and their herd of pedigree Devon cattle.

The abbey is open Good Friday–end October, Wednesday, Sunday and Bank Holidays, 1–4.30. Refreshments from 12 noon. The garden and plant nursery open daily, 10–4.30. Telephone: South Chard (01460) 20231

Mapperton Gardens
The Jacobean manor house is surrounded by Italianate terraced gardens on three levels.

Gardens open March–October, daily, 2–6. Telephone: Bridport (01308) 862645

Bear right to drive through Hooke over the crossroads and continue along the northern slopes of the valley in the direction of Higher Kingcombe. Drive over the crossroads in Higher Kingcombe signposted Great Toller. The road bears right through Lower Kingcombe then left for Toller Porcorum. Pass the church in Toller Porcorum and turn left at the T-junction signposted Maiden Newton and Dorchester. The road climbs the hillside to meet the A356. Turn left along the A356 signposted Beaminster. Follow the main road for about 6½ miles. Drive past the junction with the B3163 and take the next road on the left signposted Beaminster. At a T-junction turn left for just a few yards and then turn right signposted Mosterton **G**. The road follows the crest of Mintern's Hill and, in about a mile, there is a viewpoint and picnic area on the left. Beaminster lies below in the valley surrounded by hills.

Continue to meet the A3066. Turn left signposted Beaminster. The road runs through a tunnel and you will see the entrance to Horn Park Gardens on the right. The gardens are open to the public. **Continue along the A3066 to the centre of Beaminster.**

One of Dorset's most charming small market towns, Beaminster

BRIDPORT AND THE WEST DORSET COAST

55 MILES – 3 HOURS
START AND FINISH AT BRIDPORT

Dorset is famous for its dramatic coastal scenery and this tour visits part of the west coast to reveal some of its finest aspects. From Bridport the route follows the valley of the River Bride to its source at the enchanting village of Littlebredy before taking the coast road to Lyme Regis. Magnificent views can be enjoyed from the hill-forts crowning Eggardon Hill, Lambert's Castle Hill and Coney's Hill, and there are plenty of opportunities for cliff and downland walks.

From the centre of Bridport head east to cross the River Brit. Keep straight on at the roundabout to continue along the A35 signposted Dorchester. After about 1 1/2 miles turn right signposted Shipton Gorge and Burton Bradstock. When the road divides in the attractive village of Shipton Gorge take the right-hand road signposted Burton Bradstock. At the crossroads, turn left signposted Askerswell and, at the next crossroads bear right signposted Swyre, Puncknowle and Litton Cheney.

The lane runs south over the downs to descend into the valley of the River Bride. **Cross the river to a T-junction and turn left signposted Litton Cheney. Continue for Litton Cheney and bear right at the T-junction in the village signposted Long Bredy. Keep** to the main road through Litton Cheney. The road dips and climbs as it winds through the steep-sided downs. Medieval farmers have scored the hillsides with strip lynchets and the men of the Bronze Age have dotted the summits with their round burial mounds.

Follow the signs for Long Bredy bearing right to drive through the village. When the road divides in the village turn left signposted Littlebredy. Look right down the valley to see the white west front of Kingston Russell House. Thomas Masterman Hardy, captain of HMS *Victory* at the battle of Trafalgar, was born in this eighteenth-century mansion in 1769.

Continue for about a mile to visit one of the loveliest places in Dorset, Littlebredy. Hidden in a green valley in the downs, sheltered by huge beech trees, this tiny village in the Bridehead estate is best explored on foot. **Drive between the stone entrance pillars to the estate, past the lodge on the left, and park immediately beside the road A.** Walk ahead and turn right down the road past the shelter. Continue for about 100 yards (91 metres) and turn left through a small gate just past the first thatched house. Pass the church and walk on through the gate ahead where

The village of Littlebredy hidden away in the valley of the River Bride

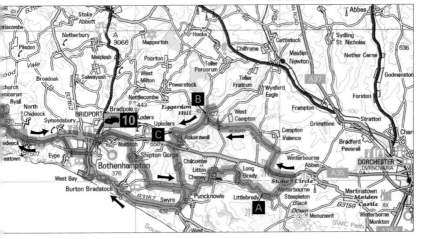

a notice invites you to enjoy a stroll in the beautiful grounds of Bridehead House. No fee is charged, but it is suggested you put a contribution in the box in the church porch.

Return to your car and continue down the road to a junction. Bear left to climb the hill out of the village. Keep ahead over the brow of the hill signposted Winterbourne Abbas and Dorchester to meet the A35. Turn left signposted Bridport. In a mile turn right signposted **Compton Valence. At the T-junction turn left to follow the line of a Roman road running high over the downs with splendid views. Keep straight on for about 5 miles signed for Eggardon Hill and Askerswell. At the crossroads turn right** **B** **signposted Toller Porcorum, then right again signposted Wynford Eagle.** Shatcombe Lane picnic area is on the left. Footpaths lead to the top of Eggardon Hill. Over 800 feet (244 metres) high it affords wonderful views south over the coastal downs to the sea.

Return to **B** **and keep straight on signposted Askerswell.** The road descends steeply. **Keep ahead over the crossroads past the Spyway Inn and after ½ mile turn left signposted Askerswell** **C**. **At the crossroads follow the main road right signposted Dorchester to run to a T-junction. Turn right to meet the A35. Cross the eastbound carriageway, turn right for a few yards and then**

• *PLACES OF INTEREST* •

Bridport

Since the Middle Ages this small market town has been England's principal producer of ropes and cord for the Royal Navy and nets to equip the fishing fleet. Hemp for the ropes and flax for the manufacture of sailcloth flourish in the rich soils of the surrounding Marshwood Vale. Traditionally, the hangman's rope was made here giving rise to the expression 'stabbed with a Bridport dagger'.

The centre of the town is predominantly Georgian with wide pavements ideal as ropewalks. Facing the square is Bridport's fine arcaded Georgian Town Hall. The chemist's shop opposite stands on the site of the old George Inn. Escaping from Cromwell's troops after his defeat at the battle of Worcester, Charles II, disguised as a groom, stopped at the George for rest and refreshment. Unfortunately for the king, the town was full of Cromwell's soldiers and he had to push his way through them to cross the inn yard to attend to the horses. The fugitives escaped down Lee Lane, a track off the Dorchester road, now marked with a stone monument to commemorate the event.

The basically thirteenth- to fifteenth-century church was restored in the nineteenth century. It contains a splendid effigy of a knight in armour.

The museum is housed in a restored Tudor building and exhibits include finds from the Roman camp near Stoke Abbot.

West Bay

From this little harbour, now a busy fishing port, rope and twine were carried throughout the world, often in ships built in the adjacent shipyard. Today it exports gravel and sand and imports timber. West Bay is an excellent starting point for coastal walks.

Chideock

Chideock is tucked snugly in a small fertile vale. It is an unspoilt old-world village with a handsome fifteenth-century church. It takes its name from the Chidiock family whose mansion once stood north of the village. The house, which was held for the king during the Civil War, was slighted in 1645 by order of Colonel Ceely, the commandant of Lyme.

51

Burton Bradstock's maze of picturesque alleyways flanked by old-world cottages is best explored on foot

turn left signposted Chilcombe. Follow the lane for about a mile and then bear left at a fork to a parking area for Chilcombe Church. Walk over the field to see unchanged Dorset. The tiny church stands beside the manor in a hollow in the hillside overlooking a small square and picturesque farm buildings. The church has a carved wooden reredos said to have come from one of the ships of the Spanish Armada cast ashore on the Chesil Beach.

Retrace the route to the fork and turn left to continue south. Keep ahead over the crossroads signposted Swyre. At the T-junction bear right then left signposted Swyre to meet the B3157. Turn right signposted Burton Bradstock. Splendid views of the coastline open ahead. Beyond the orange cliffs of Burton Bradstock are the darker cliffs fringing Lyme Bay rising to the highest point on England's south coast, Golden Cap.

Keep to the main road which turns right in Burton Bradstock, a charming village with many old thatched houses. Continue for about 1½ miles and then take the road on the left for West Bay. This small harbour is situated where the River Brit enters the sea. There is ample parking beside the harbour where fishing boats and small craft bob on the tide. Beyond the narrow harbour entrance steep sandstone cliffs rise either side of the shingle beach.

Leave the harbour and turn left signposted Bridport. At the roundabout turn left along the A35 signposted Honiton and continue following the signs for Chideock and Lyme Regis. After 3½ miles the road runs through Chideock, another of Dorset's many attractive villages, where the dark thatched roofs of the houses contrast with deep yellow sandstone walls. Continue along the A35 through Morecombelake then bear left following the signs for Charmouth. Here Dorset thatch combines happily with the elegance of a small Georgian watering place. Neat colour-washed houses front the steep High Street. At the traffic lights turn left signed for the car park by the beach. At nearby Black Ven, Mary Anning found her famous ichthyosaurus in 1811.

Retrace the route to Charmouth and turn left, then bear left for Lyme Regis along the B3052. To cut off a steep corner turn left along a lane signposted Lyme Regis to a T-junction. Turn right to rejoin the B3052 and turn left. The road descends to the seafront of this historic town bearing right past the network of narrow medieval streets beside the River Lym. A visit to the old harbour, called the Cobb, is a must! It is a little west of the town. Keep to the A3052 as it turns right at the foot of the High Street. After about 100 yards (91 metres) bear left, still following the A3052 signposted Exeter. Cross the top of Cobb Road and turn left into the car park. There is parking at the foot of Cobb Road, but this can become crowded, so it is better to leave your car in the car park and walk down Cobb Road to the harbour. Massive sea walls fling protective arms round a small sheltered corner of the bay. Walk along the sea wall to see the famous 'Granny teeth' where Jane Austen's Louisa Musgrove made her foolhardy jump to the quayside below in *Persuasion*.

Bridport's harbour, West Bay

From the car park at the top of Cobb Road look over the road and a little to your left and you will see Pound Street, signposted Uplyme and Axminster . Drive across the A3052 to follow Pound Street to meet the B3165. Turn left and continue uphill through Uplyme to meet the A35. Follow the sign for Crewkerne to cross the A35, turn right for a few yards then left still on the B3165. This beautiful road rises to follow a ridge of downland giving splendid views north-west to the Devon hills.

After about 4 miles, as you approach Lambert's Castle Hill, there is a National Trust car park on the right. The sign is difficult to spot from the road, so pass a turning to Fishpond and look for a white gravel track on the right. Turn right up the track to the car park. A footpath leads the short distance to the top of Lambert's Castle Hill giving what is believed to be the finest view in Dorset. To the south lies Portland and the waters of the Fleet confined behind Chesil Beach, to the west is the rugged Devon coast and inland rise the hills of Wiltshire and Somerset. **Return to the road and turn left.**

In about ¾ mile, just past a telephone box, turn right signposted Fishpond  and at the T-junction turn

• PLACES OF INTEREST •

Charmouth

Once a fishing village situated in a break in the steep cliffs over-looking Lyme Bay, Charmouth is now a popular seaside resort. It still retains a great deal of the charm that delighted Jane Austen. Thatched cottages and neat Regency houses with bow windows face each other across the hilly main street. The Queen's Arms hotel, dating from the beginning of the sixteenth century, welcomed Catherine of Aragon soon after her arrival in England. (The building is no longer a hotel).

The Charmouth Heritage Coast Centre on the seafront is open May–end September, daily. Telephone: Charmouth (01297) 560772

Lyme Regis

Lyme Regis enchanted Jane Austen, and today it continues to charm all who visit it. Beautifully situated in the steep-sided valley of the River Lym, the old town stands precariously balanced on its unstable blue clay, firmly buttressed against the force of the waves. Seen from the Cobb, each side of the town reveals sharply contrasting scenery. To the east runs an undulating chain of slate-blue cliffs barred by golden limestone, and to the west thickly-wooded hillsides reach almost to the water's edge.

A harbour has stood close to the town since early in the fourteenth century. From its walls the townspeople watched Drake skirmish with ships of the Armada in 1588 and, on the beach west of the Cobb, the Duke of Monmouth made his ill-fated landing in 1685.

The history of Lyme is told in detail in the museum housed in the **Town Hall** where there is also a fine collection of fossils. Open 1 April–31 October, Monday–Saturday 10–5, Sunday 10–12 and 2.30–5. Telephone: Lyme Regis (01297) 443370

right. The road runs south along the east side of Lambert's Castle Hill. **Keep straight on to the top of the hill and, at the junction, turn left signposted Wootton Fitzpaine.** As the road follows the crest of Coney's Hill there is a car park on the left beside another magnificent hill-fort with wonderful views. No walking is required to enjoy them! **Continue south to**

a T-junction and turn left signposted Whitchurch. The road descends to cross the River Char. At the crossroads turn left signposted Shave Cross to drive through Whitchurch Canonicorum. The church on the right has a fine fifteenth-century tower and is notable as the only parish church in England with a shrine containing the bones of its patron saint, St Wita. The leaden casket containing the bones was discovered in the north transept in 1900 when the foundations settled.

Follow the road as it turns right past the church and continue following the signs for Ryall. At the crossroads keep straight ahead. In Ryall the road bears right signposted Bridport to meet the A35. Turn left signposted Bridport and continue along the A35, bearing left along the B3162 to return to the town centre. ■

Boats shelter behind the massive walls of the famous Cobb at Lyme Regis

SOUTHAMPTON WATER AND THE ESTUARIES OF THE HAMBLE AND THE MEON

65 MILES – 4 HOURS
START AND FINISH AT SOUTHAMPTON

East of Southampton, along the shores of Southampton Water and the Hamble and Meon rivers, there are many discoveries to be made. Apart from the famous boating villages of Hamble and Bursledon, the route passes Westwood Woodland Park and the Royal Victoria Country Park. Visits are made to the ruins of two abbeys at Netley and Titchfield plus the remains of the palace at Bishop's Waltham. The tour returns past Marwell Zoological Park, set in more than one hundred acres of attractive countryside.

A small toll is payable to cross the bridge over the River Itchen in Southampton.

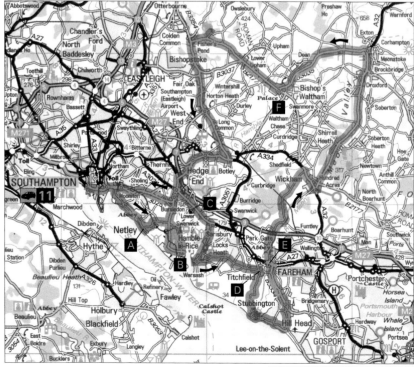

SCALE 1:250 000 OR 1 INCH TO 4 MILES 1 CM TO 2.5 KM

Leave Southampton Town Quay heading east along the A33 signed Fareham and Portsmouth. The road turns left then right round Queens Park. Turn right for Ocean Village and follow the road as it bears left past the entrance to Ocean Village on the right. At the second set of traffic lights turn left signed Woolston via Toll Bridge. At the roundabout turn right to cross the bridge over the River Itchen. Go through the toll barriers to a roundabout. Turn hard right signed Woolston and Bitterne. At the traffic lights turn left and then continue for about ¼ mile. Opposite the Ship Inn turn left signed Weston Shore and Netley. The road runs down to the shore of Southampton Water at Weston Hard. There is a car park here giving a view of this great seaway from the western docks to Calshot Spit.

Follow the road as it turns left signed Netley Abbey. Continue along the shore for about a mile to another car park on the right, opposite

The medieval Bargate, Southampton

an entrance to Westwood Woodland Park. Signposted paths lead through old pasture woodland rich in wild flowers.

Continue past Westwood towards Netley. On the left is the car park beside the ruins of Netley Abbey. These romantic ruins, set in a shallow valley, date from 1239 when, at the request of the Bishop of Winchester, Cistercian monks from Beaulieu established a sister house here by the waterside. Graceful thirteenth-century work remains in the stone of the arches and windows of the former abbey church.

Keep straight on to drive through Netley. When the main road turns left signed Bursledon and Hamble **A** keep ahead to the Royal Victoria Country Park where there is ample parking. Only the chapel of the great military hospital that once stood in these beautifully landscaped grounds has been preserved. It is now a museum housing displays revealing the history of the hospital since its foundation shortly after the Crimean war. From the dome you can enjoy views of Southampton Water.

• PLACES OF INTEREST •

Southampton
There is so much to say about this great commercial seaport that it is impossible to include details here. A section has been devoted to Southampton in the Introduction (page 7).

For further information contact the Tourist Information Centre, Above Bar Precinct. Telephone: Southampton (01703) 221106

Westwood Woodland Park
To walk through Westwood is to step back in time 800 years. The landscape has changed little since it belonged to Netley Abbey and was worked by Cistercian monks. The Westwood Rangers have cared for Westwood since 1987.

For details of many organised activities contact the Westwood

office. Open normal office hours and most weekends. Telephone: Southampton (01703) 456484. Westwood is always open and parking is free.

Netley Abbey
After the Dissolution of the monasteries the estate was granted to Sir William Paulet who converted the abbey into a mansion. The south transept became a great hall with a screened-off kitchen. It is said he used the nave of the church as a tennis court and stabled his horses in the monks' refectory! The mansion was inhabited until 1700, but now only traces of the brickwork remain.

Open Easter–end September, 10–1 and 2–6. Rest of year weekends only until 4.

Royal Victoria Country Park, Netley
The hospital saw service throughout the Boer War and the two world wars. It was one of the main centres of the Royal Army Medical Corps, and the laboratories contributed much to medical research.

In the First World War, Netley became No 1 base hospital. In 1942 the hospital was taken over by the Americans, who are said to have driven jeeps up its ¼-mile-long corridors! Hampshire County Council purchased the site in 1980.

Grounds open throughout the year. Chapel and tearooms open Easter–September. Telephone: Southampton (01703) 455157

Hamble village is famous throughout the world as a yachting centre

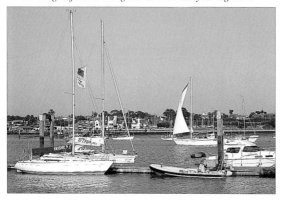

Return to the main road at and turn right. Keep to the main road following the signs for Hamble. Cross the railway and continue to meet the B3397. Turn right signposted Hamble Village. Drive through the village to a large car park on the left. As the road is narrow, it is advisable to leave your car here and walk down to the quay. However, there is parking on the quay. This is a perfect place to take a break. Every kind of craft can be seen thronging the river – from yachts built to the latest design to old timers, from ocean racers to fishing boats.

Return to your car and turn left down Satchell Lane. Follow the lane as it curves past the former airfield to meet the the B3397 at a T-junction. Turn right along the B3397 which joins the A3025. Continue ahead following signs for Bursledon. Cross two small roundabouts to meet the A27 at a large roundabout. Bear right following the signs for Sarisbury A27 (not West End A27). Continue for a little over a mile.

Just before the railway bridge in Bursledon, turn right signposted for the station and free car park. The car park is by the station on the left. A marked footpath leads uphill into Old Bursledon. Many warships were built here

during the fourteenth, fifteenth and sixteenth centuries, including the *Elephant*, Nelson's flagship at the battle of Copenhagen. Old Bursledon is a conservation area with many elegant seventeenth- and eighteenth-century houses.

Return to the A27 at . Turn right to cross the River Hamble. Continue for a mile, then turn right signposted Warsash. At the T-junction bear right for Warsash to run to the crossroads in the centre of Warsash village. Turn right signposted Fore-shore and Public Hard to drive down to the waterfront car park in front of the Rising Sun Inn. The cottages here are a reminder of the days when this was a small fishing village noted for its crabs and lobsters. There is a memorial here to the men who took part in the D-Day landings. The round black and white tower is the Harbour Master's office. **From the car park continue along the waterfront leaving the Rising Sun on your right to follow the one-way system. Bear left to return to the crossroads in the centre of Warsash village.**

Drive straight across signed Titchfield and Fare-ham. Keep to the main road as it curves left past a church. Continue for about 2 miles towards Titchfield. At the next junction bear right signed Titchfield 1 mile. Keep on for about ¼ mile and be ready to

turn right down Posbrook Lane signposted Meon . (The sign is on your left before you turn right). The lane leads to parking areas on the Meon Shore at Titch-field Haven. From here there is a splendid view over the Solent to the Isle of Wight. In 1611, Shakespeare's patron, the third Earl of Southampton, blocked the mouth of the River Meon and built a canal from Titchfield village to the sea. The blocked estuary is now a nature reserve.

Continue from the parking area round the harbour at Hill Head. Drive through the village and, at the T-junction, turn left signposted Stubbing-ton and Lee-on-the-Solent. At the next T-junction turn left and continue for about a mile to meet the B3334. Turn left and continue following the signs for Titchfield. At the traffic lights do not turn left for Titchfield village, but continue straight ahead to meet the A27. Turn left signed Southampton. After a few yards turn right following the sign (on the left of the road) for Titchfield Abbey. The road runs past the entrance on the left to Place House and the abbey ruins.

Keep to the main road as it runs under the motorway (M27) and along the west bank of the River Meon to meet the A334. Turn right signposted Wickham. Drive into the village, under the railway and, at the round-about, turn left along the A32 for Alton and Droxford. Continue along the A32 over the crossroads towards Alton. The road runs through the Forest of Bere to Droxford. In the railway station – now disused – Eisenhower, Churchill and other Allied leaders planned the D-Day landings.

Continue along the A32, past Meonstoke and its church, to Corhampton. This tiny village possesses one

Titchfield Haven Nature Reserve

Permits are required to visit the hides, but a signed footpath can be followed from the parking area close to the sea mark.

To obtain a permit write to The Naturalist Warden, Haven Cottage, Cliff Road, Hill Head, Fareham, Hampshire. Telephone: Fareham (01329) 662145

Titchfield Abbey, Place House and Tithe Barn

The abbey was a house of Premonstratensian Canons who took their name from the monastery of Prémontré in France. For 300 years it was the centre of life at the head of the Meon estuary. Outstanding among the abbey ruins is the entrance to the chapter house and part of the cloisters. After the Dissolution the abbey was remodelled as a stately home by Thomas Wriothesley, who finished building Place House in 1542. The gatehouse, which survives today, was built across the nave of the abbey church. Wriothesley was later created first Earl of Southampton. His grandson was Shakespeare's patron, the golden haired young man in the Sonnets, and it is possible that a performance of *Romeo and Juliet* took place in the great tithe barn. The house was demolished in the eighteenth century.

The ruins are open Good Friday–30 September, 10–1 and 2–6. Telephone: Fareham (01329) 643016

Bishop's Waltham Palace

The ruins include the Great Hall and the three-storey tower. The ground floor of the Dower House is furnished as a nineteenth-century farmhouse.

Open 1 April–30 September, daily, 10–6. Telephone: Bishop's Waltham (01489) 892460

Marwell Zoological Park

Marwell specialises in the care of endangered species, including the scimitar horned oryx and the Przewalski horse, and big cats such as Asian lions, Siberian tigers and snow leopards. Picnic areas and refreshments. Open daily (except Christmas Day) from 10–6 (5 in winter). Telephone: Winchester (01962) 777406

of Hampshire's treasures – a wonderfully preserved Saxon church. **Turn left along the B3035 signed for Bishop's Waltham and, almost immediately, turn right up a narrow gravel entry to the parking area.** Follow the footpath to the church. This small church has remained almost unaltered since it was built early in the eleventh century. Inside, the most striking feature is the perfect Saxon chancel arch.

Turn right from the parking area to continue

The ruins of Bishop's Waltham Palace. This fortified medieval palace was destroyed in 1644 during the Civil War.

in the direction of Bishop's Waltham. A pleasant drive through undulating, well-wooded countryside brings you to a roundabout in Bishop's Waltham. Turn left **F** following the sign for Bishop's Waltham Palace. After a few yards turn right following the next sign for the palace to the car park.

Turn left from the car park to return to the roundabout at **F**. Keep ahead on the B2177 following the signs for Eastleigh and Winchester, and the brown sign for Marwell Zoological Park. After about 1½ miles turn right signed for the Park. The entrance is on the left.

Turn right from the car park to return to the main road, the B2177. Turn right to meet the B3354 and then left following the signs to Botley. After about 4 miles, at the crossroads in the village, turn right along the A334 signed Southampton. After about a mile leave the A334 and bear left along the B3033 signed Hedge End. Keep ahead for about ¾ mile. At the roundabout turn left signed Bursledon and Hamble. Keep to the B3033 as it bridges the motorway to meet the A27. Turn left along the A27 to run up to a large roundabout. Follow the signs for Hamble, Lowford and Netley, past the exits for the motorway and the A27 for Fareham and bear left signed Lowford and Netley. At the next two roundabouts keep ahead for Hamble. Do not continue to the village, but turn right following the sign for Woolston. Bear right under the railway bridge to drive through Woolston. Keep ahead at the roundabout to recross the Itchen Toll Bridge. Turn left signed Old Town and Waterfront and, at the traffic lights, turn right to return to Town Quay. ■

OLD PORTSMOUTH, THE PETERSFIELD DOWNS AND THE UPPER MEON VALLEY

65 MILES – 3½ HOURS
START AND FINISH AT GRAND PARADE, OLD PORTSMOUTH
ALLOW TWO DAYS, IF POSSIBLE, FOR THIS LONG TOUR

From Grand Parade, at the foot of Old Portsmouth High Street, the route follows the coast past Southsea Castle and then heads north to the bird sanctuary at Farlington Marshes. This is followed by a visit to the Queen Elizabeth Country Park and a tour of the beautiful downs north of Petersfield. The return route visits some of the pretty villages in the Meon valley, including East and West Meon and Hambledon, famous as the village where the rules of cricket were devised. The tour ends with a visit to the magnificent ruins of Portchester Castle.

The starting point for this tour is Grand Parade in Old Portsmouth. Approaching Portsmouth from the north follow the signs for the Historic Ships and then the signs for the A3 and Old Portsmouth. At the foot of Old Portsmouth High Street the A3 turns right with the ramparts on the left. Just before the turn, the large parking area in Grand Parade is signed for the Garrison Church on the left. If this car park is full there is an alternative pay car park opposite Southsea funfair. From here you

• *PLACES OF INTEREST* •

Portsmouth
There is so much to say about Portsmouth, the home of the Royal Navy, that it is impossible to include details here. A section has been devoted to this city in the introduction (pages 6 and 7). For further information contact the Tourist Information Centre, The Hard, Hampshire, telephone (01705) 826722 or 102 Commercial Road, Hampshire, telephone: (01705) 838382.

Sea Life Centre, Southsea
A wide variety of marine life can be seen in large tanks providing authentic habitat. Coffee shop and restaurant. Open daily. Telephone: Portsmouth (01705) 734461

D-Day Museum, Southsea
The events of D-Day and the months of preparation beforehand are told with films, displays and tableaux. The distinctive circular building houses the remarkably accurate and detailed Overlord Embroidery. The embroidery is 274 feet (84 metres) in length, 41 feet (12.5 metres) longer than the Bayeux tapestry. The thirty-four panels are based on contemporary photographs. Open April–October, 10–5.30. November–March, 10–4.30. Telephone: Portsmouth (01705) 827261

Southsea Castle
Although the guns of this Tudor fortress have never fired a shot in anger, it has had an eventful history which is illustrated in a succession of fascinating tableaux. From its battlements Henry VIII watched the pride of the English Fleet, the *Mary Rose*, heel over and sink on her way to fight the French. During the Civil War the castle was held for the King. It was manned during both world wars but was released by the Ministry of Defence in 1960. Children especially will be intrigued by an underground tunnel.
Open March–October, daily, 10–5.30. November–February, daily, 10–4.30. Telephone: (01705) 827261

Farlington Marshes
A magical place, especially in winter, when great flocks of Brent geese arrive from the Arctic to feed on the eel grass and rough pastures. The marshes are cared for by the Hampshire and Isle of Wight Naturalists' Trust. Telephone: (01794) 513786 or 830070

can take a signposted walk to Old Portsmouth of just over 1/2 mile. **Turn right from Grand Parade, up Old Portsmouth High Street. Continue for only 100 yards (91 metres) and then take the first road on the right, Pembroke Road, opposite the cathedral. Keep ahead to a roundabout and turn right. Bear left at the next roundabout, then left again opposite the Hovercraft terminal to drive east by the seafront along Clarence Esplanade.** You pass Southsea Common on the left and the Sea Life Centre and the D-Day Museum on the right. A road on the right leads to Southsea Castle. **At the next junction, past South Parade Pier, bear right to continue along the seafront. After about 1/2 mile look carefully for a turning on the left, signposted Out of City A, along the A288. The road doglegs right then left. At the roundabout keep ahead still following the A288. Bear right at the traffic lights at the junction with the A2030 and, in just over 1/2 mile, turn right at the next roundabout, still following the A2030 signposted Out of City.**

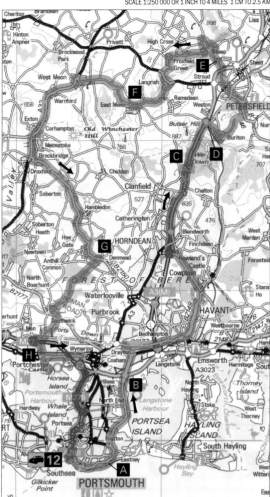

The road runs north along the western shore of Langstone Harbour. **This is where you need to navigate carefully. Cross Ports Creek to a roundabout under the A27. Get into the right-hand lane. Drive almost all the way**

Walkers enjoy a stroll in the Queen Elizabeth Country Park

round the roundabout, under the A27, but just before you complete the circle, look carefully for the small slip road on the left signed on a green board Farlington Marshes car park B. Turn left to park.** A short walk along the sea wall will be rewarded by a wealth of wild flowers and sea birds. **Return to your car and turn left from the entrance to the marshes to rejoin the roundabout. Take the third exit to continue north along the A2030 signed Farlington.**

Look out for a sign indicating a left turn for Cosham and, at the T-junction, turn left as directed. After only 50 yards (46 metres), turn

right up Farlington Avenue to climb Portsdown Hill and meet the B2177. Turn right along the B2177 signposted a little further on for Bedhampton and Havant.** The road runs high along the top of Portsdown Hill giving splendid views over Portsmouth Harbour. **Follow the B2177 over the A3(M) to a roundabout. Keep ahead still on the B2177 signposted Havant. At the traffic lights at the junction with the B2150 bear right for 1/4 mile. At the roundabout turn left along the B2149 signposted Havant. At the next roundabout turn left still following the B2149 signposted Rowland's Castle**

Stoner Hill, near Steep, was the inspiration for some of Edward Thomas's finest poetry

and Staunton Country Park. The entrance to Staunton Country Park is on the left.

After visiting the park rejoin the B2149, turn left and continue for about 1¹/₂ miles. At the roundabout follow signs for A3(M) London and Petersfield to join the A3(M) heading north. Shortly after, the motorway becomes the A3. Continue north along the A3 and, in a little more than 2 miles, a brown sign on the left indicates the road to Butser Ancient Farm **C**. **If you would like to visit the site turn left and follow the signs.**

After your visit rejoin the A3 and continue north for about ¹/₂ mile and then turn left to follow the signs to the Queen Elizabeth Country Park and Visitor Centre. Find time if you can to walk to Butser Hill, the highest point of the South Downs giving wonderful views.

Follow the exit signs from the car park and bear right for Petersfield. The road then bears left to rejoin the A3. Continue north for about a mile and then bear left following the sign for Petersfield. The road bears right for Petersfield under the A3 to a roundabout **D**. **Keep ahead for Buriton.**

Follow the lane through pretty wooded country over the crossroads into this attractive village built of cream-coloured stone. Pass the pond on your right and turn left in front of the church along North Lane. Keep to the main road to meet the B2146. Turn left signposted Petersfield. Bear left past the junction with the B2199. A car park on the right gives access to Petersfield Heath, a delightful area of countryside with footpaths encircling a large lake. **Pass the lake on your right and continue straight over the crossroads.** If you would like to explore Petersfield turn right at the crossroads to the High Street where you will find car parks. **The road bears right, signposted on the corner A272 Winchester, to meet the A272. Turn left signposted Winchester and keep ahead over the level-crossing to a roundabout. Take the second exit signposted Steep and Froxfield.**

The road runs north to a crossroads in Steep E (unsigned). Make a detour here and turn right to see the village. The trees 'above the inn, the smithy and the shop' inspired Edward Thomas's poem *Aspens*. The little Norman church on the

right has a beautiful engraved glass window in the poet's memory. The poet came to live in Steep in 1913, first at Berryfield Cottage, then at Yew Tree Cottage near the church.

Retrace the route to the crossroads at E and turn right to climb the beautifully wooded slopes of Shoulder of Mutton Hill. A Sarsen Stone dedicating the area to Edward Thomas has been placed on the hillside. **If you would like to see the stone (involving a walk of about ¹/₂ mile) turn right as you leave the trees at the top of the hill down Cockshott Lane. Drive for about 50 yards (46 metres) then pull off the road into one of the parking areas.** Walk on down the lane and keep ahead along the track when the metalling ceases. Follow the footpath sign on the right. Ignore footpaths to left and right and keep straight ahead downhill to the Sarsen Stone which is in a clearing. The stone is inscribed 'And I rose up, and knew I was tired, and continued my journey.' The view across the Hampshire border to the Sussex Downs is breathtaking.

Retrace the route down Cockshott Lane and turn right. After a few yards the road divides. Bear left signposted High Cross and Privett to a crossroads. Turn left signposted Froxfield Green and Langrish. The road turns right to a junction in Froxfield Green. Follow the main road as it bears left for Langrish. The road then bears right for Langrish to meet the A272. Turn left signposted Langrish and after ³/₄ mile, in the village, downhill on the bend, turn right signposted East Meon. A few yards further on turn right again for East Meon. The road now runs beside the River Meon, through one of the loveliest valleys in Hampshire, to East Meon. **Turn left opposite the church F**

• PLACES OF INTEREST •

Staunton Country Park
The park contains all the features of a country estate apart from the house – walled gardens, the home farm, Victorian glasshouses, coach house and stables.

Open April–October, 10–5. Rest of year 10–4. Telephone: Havant (01705) 453405

Queen Elizabeth Country Park
One of the finest country parks in the British Isles covering more than 1,000 acres of dramatic scenery ranging from high open downland with deep combes to beech forests. The Park Centre has an audio-visual theatre, an informative display, a craft centre and a shop for souvenirs and guidebooks. Refreshments are available in the Coach House Café.

An underpass leads to Butser Ancient Farm, a reconstruction of an Iron Age settlement. A country fair is held in July. There are sheep-dog trials, show ground events and stands for countryside organisations.

The park is open at all times. The centre is open March–October, daily, 10–5. Weekends only, November–December. Sunday only January and February.

Telephone: Portsmouth (01705) 595040

Petersfield
The Church of St Peter dates from the twelfth century and has a splendid Norman chancel arch.

The Church Path Studio in the Square has a charming gallery displaying the work of the pre-war Petersfield artist, Flora Twort. There is also a restaurant. Open Tuesday–Saturday, 9.30–5. Closed part of February. Telephone: Petersfield (01730) 260756

Portchester Castle
This impressive castle, at the head of Portsmouth Harbour, has a history reaching back to the Romans who anchored their galleys beside its walls. The Norman keep was a residence for kings in times past and a prison for French captives during the Napoleonic wars. In the lower storey is an exhibition illustrating the castle's long history.

Open daily. April–September, 10–6. October–March, 10–4. Closed December 24–26 and January 1. Telephone: Portsmouth (01705) 378291

and follow the signs to the car park. This delightful village has a magnificent Norman church and fifteenth-century Court House.

Retrace your route to **F** and turn left to follow the road to meet the A32 in West Meon. Turn left along the A32 signposted Droxfield

and Fareham. Follow the river valley, bearing left at the junction with the B3035, to continue past turnings to Corhampton and Meonstoke. After about a mile, turn left along the B2150 signposted Waterlooville and Hambledon. Follow the

road through Hambledon, another attractive village. A monument opposite the Bat and Ball Inn commemorates the village's associations with cricket.

Continue south along the B2150 signposted Denmead. After about 2½ miles, in Denmead, turn right just past the White Hart Inn, then right again for Southwick **G**. At the roundabout keep ahead for Southwick. The road runs through Creech Woods, part of the medieval Forest of Bere. A car park on the left gives access to picnic areas and forest trails. Follow the road to Southwick. At the junction in Southwick turn left signposted Wickham and Portsmouth and continue past the church on the left to a T-junction. Turn right to a roundabout. Keep ahead signposted Portchester. Follow the main road as it bears left to a crossroads. Go straight over the crossroads. There is now a marvellous view over Portsmouth Harbour. After about 50 yards (46 metres) there is a large parking area on the left (unsigned) where you can stop to enjoy the view. Keep to the main road as it bears left to cross the M27 to a roundabout on the A27 **H**. Keep ahead following the brown signs for Portchester Castle and drive down to the castle's car parks on either side of the road.

After visiting the castle retrace the route to the A27 at **H**. Turn right signposted Portsmouth and keep straight on under the motorway. At the roundabout follow the signs for Portsmouth, M27 and M275. Bear left following the M275 for Portsmouth. Follow the signs for the Historic Ships and then the signs for the A3 and Old Portsmouth. Continue down Old Portsmouth High Street and turn left into Grand Parade signed for the Garrison Church. ■

The massive walls of Portchester Castle date from Roman times

ROMSEY AND THE TEST VALLEY

50 MILES – 3 HOURS
START AND FINISH AT ROMSEY

The small town of Romsey, clustered around its ancient abbey beside the River Test, makes a perfect introduction to this tour. The route follows the Test valley past Mottisfont, famous for its abbey and rose garden, and through old-world villages of thatched, half-timbered cottages. It then crosses the high downland north-west of Romsey to the magnificent Iron Age fort on Danebury Hill before returning through the tiny village of East Wellow, where Florence Nightingale is buried. Visits are made to the Museum of Army Flying at Middle Wallop, the Hawk Conservancy on the slopes of Weyhill, and Broadlands, the home of Lord and Lady Romsey.

Leave Romsey heading north up the Test valley along the A3057 signposted Stockbridge. The clear waters of this famous trout stream run through lush meadows framed by low wooded hills. The road crosses the river and then runs along the east side of the valley, through Timsbury. **Continue past the Bear and Ragged Staff pub and, in about ½ mile, turn left signposted Mottisfont A. Follow the road as it bears right over the river and turn right into the**

Wherwell, beside the River Test, is an enchanting Hampshire village

car park for Mottisfont Abbey Gardens. You can walk from the car park to the abbey which is surrounded by lawns shaded by magnificent trees and threaded by the River Test and a stream rising from a spring in the grounds.

To continue the tour retrace the route to the A3057 at A. Turn left signposted King's Somborne and follow the valley for 3 miles to the village. King John is said to have hunted here.

Drive through King's Somborne to follow the A3057 to Stockbridge. This is a market town of predominantly Tudor and Georgian houses, built beside an old drovers' road. The National Trust became Lord of the Manor of Stockbridge in 1946 and, with the lordship, it acquired Stockbridge Down, a chalk hill rich in plants and shrubs east of the town. **To see the down, turn left as you approach the town to a large roundabout. Take the third exit signposted for Winchester. After a mile you will pass a parking area on the right. Drive on for about ¾ mile and, just over the crest of a small hill, there is a car park on the left giving access to the down. The sign is not visible from the road so look carefully for the narrow asphalted entry surmounted by a height-limiting bar.** A footpath leads up the down, fragrant with wild thyme, to the embankments of Woolbury Iron Age fort offering spectacular views.

Retrace the route to the roundabout at Stockbridge and turn right signposted Andover to continue north along the A3057 through Leckford. After a mile, when the A3057 turns left, keep ahead (watch for traffic) signposted Chilbolton. Immediately past the corner, West Down car park is on the right. It is beside a prehistoric road, the Mark Way, which leads to West Down. Groups of ancient

Romsey

This delectable little town is famous for its splendid abbey which has been described as 'music in stone'. Dating from the early twelfth century, and completed within 130 years, the Norman and Early English styles are in perfect harmony with no detail out of place. An earlier Saxon church stood on the site, built as part of a monastic complex for nuns, and the foundations can still be seen beneath a trapdoor. The nuns were fine teachers and among their pupils were the daughters of the Scots king, Malcolm. At the Dissolution the monastic buildings were destroyed except for the refectory, and the church was bought by the townspeople for £100. The interior is magnificent. Most impressive is the Norman nave which is over 250 feet (76 metres) in length and rises to a height of over 70 feet (21 metres). Among many treasures is an Anglo-Saxon rood, an early sixteenth-century painted reredos, fourteenth-century tiles and some exquisite modern tapestries. Today, visitors from throughout the world pay their last respects to Lord Louis, Earl Mountbatten of Burma, who is buried in the abbey close to his family pew.

Romsey's oldest house, **King John's House**, stands close to the abbey. It was built in about 1240 for a merchant, but in its time has served as a king's residence and a workhouse. It is now a museum and centre for cultural activities. The garden is laid out to reflect the age of the house. Open Spring Bank Holiday–end September, 10.30–12.30 and 2–4. Closed Sunday and Monday mornings. Telephone: Romsey (01794) 512200

Mottisfont Abbey and Gardens
Enclosed within a walled garden is the National Trust's collection of old roses, at their best in late June and July, but skillfully underplanted to provide interest from April to September.

Open 1 April–end of October, Saturday–Wednesday, 12–6 or dusk if earlier. June, Saturday–Thursday, 12–8.30. Gift shop. Special events are organised. Telephone: Romsey (01794) 341220

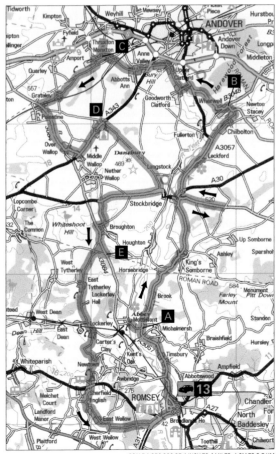

SCALE 1:250 000 OR 1 INCH TO 4 MILES *1 CM TO 2.5 KM*

pit dwellings, Celtic pottery and flint scrapers have been found here. **Keep on for Chilbolton, pass the pub in the village and, at the road junction, turn left signposted Wherwell. The road doglegs right then left to meet the B3420. Turn left signposted Wherwell to cross the meandering streams of the River Test to meet the B3048. Turn left, signposted Andover, for Wherwell.** This is an enchanting village of thatched, white-walled cottages. **To stop and explore turn left just before the cenotaph B and drive down the lane towards the church to a car park on the left.** In medieval times life revolved around Wherwell Priory, established on the site of the present church in AD 986 by Queen Elfrida, widow of King Edgar, to ease her conscience after murdering her stepson at Corfe.

Return to the cenotaph at B and turn left. Continue for about 100 yards (91 metres) and then follow the road right at the crossroads, along the B3420 signposted Andover. When you meet

the A3057 turn right signposted Andover. In just over ¼ mile turn left signposted Goodworth Clatford. Pass the church and cross the River Anton to a T-junction in the village. Turn right signposted Upper Clatford and Abbotts Ann. The road bears left signposted Anna Valley and Abbotts Ann, then right for a few yards. The road now bears left again signposted Abbotts Ann. Drive through Anna Valley to meet the A343. Turn left signposted Salisbury. After ¼ mile turn right signposted Little Ann. Continue past the Abbotts Ann village sign and follow the road as it bears left, still signposted Abbotts Ann. Almost immediately, there is a car park on the left opposite the church. The medieval custom of carrying white paper garlands at the funerals of maidens and bachelors has been observed in the village, and many garlands dating back to the early eighteenth century hang on the church walls.

Past the church in Abbotts Ann the road turns right and, after about 100 yards (91 metres), runs to a T-junction. Turn right and then, almost immediately left, signposted Monxton. Cross the railway and drive over the crossroads into Monxton village. Pass the church and the inn and take the next road on the right, Sarson Lane **C**. After about ¾ mile look carefully for the entrance to the Hawk Conservancy which is on the left. This large collection of birds of prey includes eagles, owls and kites, and provides an opportunity to observe these beautiful birds at close hand.

Return down the lane to **C** and turn right for Amport. This is another attractive stream-side village with thatched cottages facing a green. **Drive through Amport to meet a T-junction.**

• PLACES OF INTEREST •

Hawk Conservancy, Weyhill
Weather permitting, there are regular demonstrations of the birds in flight. Open every day from 1 March–last Sunday in October, from 10.30. Café. Telephone: Andover (01264) 772252

Museum of Army Flying, Middle Wallop
Although strategic transport and air support on the battle-field are provided by the RAF, the Army keeps its own aeroplanes and helicopters for tactical reconnaissance and communications flights. The Army Air Corps has its headquarters here at Middle Wallop and runs its own flying training school.

The museum is open daily, 10–4.30. Closed 21–28 December. Restaurant. Telephone: Andover (01264) 384421

Broadlands, Romsey
Beautifully sited above green lawns bordered by the River Test, Broadlands is one of the finest houses in Hampshire. The original sixteenth-century house was transformed in the mid-eighteenth century into a graceful Palladian mansion by Lord Palmerston, the father of the great Victorian prime minister, from designs by Lancelot 'Capability' Brown and Henry Holland. The interior is equally elegant and contains many fine paintings. The furniture, porcelain and sculpture was collected by the 2nd Viscount Palmerston.

Lord Mountbatten opened Broadlands to the public in 1979, shortly before he was killed. As a tribute to his grandfather the present owner, Lord Romsey, has established the Mountbatten Exhibition. The visit begins with an audio-visual film giving an overall picture of Mountbatten's life as a sailor, statesman and commander. The exhibits include a collection of his personal possessions and photographs, the uniforms and decorations he was awarded, and the trophies, mementoes and gifts he received throughout his varied career.

There are picnic tables in the grounds, a café and gift shops. Open 1 July–31 August, 12–5.30. Telephone: Romsey (01794) 517888

Turn left and continue to another T-junction and turn right. Continue over the crossroads towards Grateley. In the village keep to the main road as it bears left to a T-junction. Bear left here still following the main road as it runs to meet the B3084. Turn left along the B3084 signposted The Wallops to cross the railway. Keep straight on for Over Wallop. Continue through Over Wallop to meet the A343 in Middle Wallop. Turn left signposted Andover. After about a mile the Museum of Army Flying is on the right.

The route now heads for **Danebury Hill Fort. This has been well signed up to this point but, at the time of** writing, the sign here is missing! Continue past the camp, over the roundabout

The grave of Florence Nightingale in St Margaret's churchyard, East Wellow

Romsey Abbey, dating from the tenth century

and, immediately after the petrol station on the right, turn right down an unsign-posted road **D**. Continue for about 2 miles to Danebury Hill Fort, signposted on the right. Turn right up the track to the car park. The hill is crowned by the most impressive Iron Age fort in Hampshire. Around 13 acres are enclosed by earthworks, banks and ditches. Extensive excavations have revealed the foundations of streets, buildings and workshops.

Retrace the route to the road and turn right to continue to meet the A30 on the western slopes of the Test valley. Turn right for, and drive west towards, the Wallop valley. Ignore the first turning on the left signposted Broughton and continue to descend into the valley to a crossroads just before the Wallop Brook. Turn left signposted Broughton to follow the road along the valley. Keep to the main road as it bears right and then left for Romsey into Broughton village. In the centre of the village turn right signposted Tytherley and Romsey to meet the B3084. Turn left signposted Romsey. Continue for about a mile then turn right signposted East and

West Tytherley **E**. **Keep to the main road as it bears left to a T-junction in East Tytherley. Turn left signposted Romsey and Lockerley. Continue south to cross the River Dun and pass the church in Lockerley.** The road runs under the railway and through Butts Green. **After about a mile turn right signposted Carter's Clay and Sherfield English. Continue for 1¹/₂ miles along the main road to meet the A27. Drive straight over following the unsignposted road ahead.** Take care here as this is a narrow road with passing places. **In about a mile turn left signposted Wellow Church.**

Follow the lane for about ¹/₂ mile and then turn right following the sign for St Margaret's Church Wellow. Follow the track past the little church to a car park. Florence Nightingale lived at nearby Embley Park, now a school, and you will find her grave, the memorial marked simply with her initials F. N., in the churchyard. The church is homely and charming. The heavily timbered roof of the thirteenth-century nave and chancel is supported by five massive wooden pillars and the walls are decorated with paintings of St Christopher and St Margaret. Follow the footpath opposite the church for a delightful short walk down to the Wellow stream.

Return to the road, turn right and continue to a T-junction. Turn right for about ¹/₄ mile and then turn left signposted Romsey. Keep on past the drive to Embley Park on the left to an off-set crossroads. The route is ahead, but it is necessary to turn left for a few yards and then right signposted Romsey. Continue to meet the A31 and then turn left to drive towards Romsey. On the right you pass the entrance to Broadlands, once the home of former Prime Minister Palmerston and Lord Mountbatten, which you may like to visit before returning to the town. ■

Broadlands, the stately home of Lord and Lady Romsey

WINCHESTER, THE BOURNE VALLEY AND THE NORTH HAMPSHIRE DOWNS

65 MILES – 4 HOURS
START AND FINISH AT WINCHESTER

Some of the most beautiful countryside in the south of England can be enjoyed on this tour. From Winchester the route runs to Farley Mount Country Park, which covers more than a thousand acres of open downland and ancient woodland. The route then heads north along the Bourne valley, dotted with old-world villages, to the steep northern downs known as the 'Hampshire Highlands'. There is an opportunity to visit Highclere Castle as the tour returns to Winchester via Watership Down and the charming Dever valley.

The tour starts from the main entrance to Winchester railway station. With the entrance on your right, turn left following the one-way system. Turn left again following the 'All routes' sign. At the traffic lights turn left signed Salisbury A30. The road runs under the railway. At the roundabout bear right along the A272 signposted Stockbridge. After ½ mile

turn left signposted Romsey (A31). Continue for about ¾ mile and then look carefully for a road on the right, Sarum Road, signposted for the private hospital and golf club **A**. Turn right here. This attractive tree-shaded lane is the route of a Roman road which once linked Winchester with Old Sarum near Salisbury.
 Follow the lane for about 2 miles to a crossroads **B**.

Drive straight over to Farley Mount Country Park. Several car parks offer opportunities to stop and enjoy the beautiful countryside. If you continue to Junction car park, you can follow footpaths up Beacon Hill from where there are glorious views over a patchwork of fields, woods and undulating downland.
 Retrace the route to the crossroads at **B** and turn left signposted Sparsholt.

· PLACES OF INTEREST ·

Winchester
The city lies in a hollow of the downs beside the River Itchen. It was an important Roman town, *Venta Belgarum*, the capital of Wessex under the Saxons and, in Alfred's time, a centre of learning. It possesses a great wealth of historical buildings, but its glory is the magnificent cathedral which dates from 1079, although it reflects all styles of architecture up to the fourteenth century. It is impossible to list all the cathedral's treasures here, but mention must be made of the splendid twelfth-century black

marble font from Tournai, the richly-carved chantry chapels, the paintings in the thirteenth-century Lady Chapel, the lively wood carvings on the choir stalls and the twelfth-century illuminated Winchester Bible. Coffers contain the bones of Saxon and Danish kings and there are many interesting tombs, including those of Izaak Walton and Jane Austen. The cathedral is the focal point of religious life in Hampshire.
 William the Conqueror built a castle here, but only the Great Hall has survived. This houses the much-discussed round table

of King Arthur. The ruins of twelfth-century Wolvesey Castle are near the present Bishop's Palace, and close by are parts of the city walls. In 1382 William of Wykeham founded Winchester College, and much of the original building remains.
 There is room here only to mention a few of Winchester's attractions. This fascinating city has a great deal more to offer. For all details contact the Tourist Information Office in the Guildhall. Telephone: (01962) 840500 or 848180

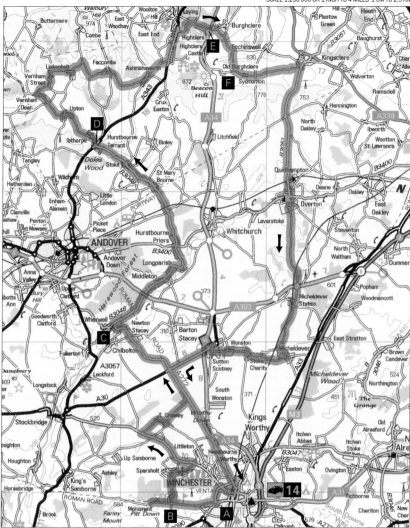

The road runs through Crab Wood, an ancient coppice woodland and a favourite place for smugglers to hide illicit goods in times past.

In Sparsholt village keep to the main road as it bears right in front of the church and right again past the Plough Inn. After about ³/₄ mile the road meets the B3049. Turn left signposted Stockbridge. Ignore the first lane on the right, and the second lane signposted Crawley, but turn right at the next lane signposted Crawley. Pass Crawley Court and keep to the main road as it bears

right through the village to a T-junction. Turn left signposted Sutton Scotney and Andover. Continue for about 1¹/₂ miles to meet the A272. Turn left signposted Andover. The road runs for about 1¹/₂ miles to meet the A30 at an off-set junction. Turn right for a few yards and then left to continue along the B3420 signposted Andover and Wherwell. Keep to the B3420 as it runs towards the valley of the River Test. The road turns left and then right to cross the river's meandering streams to meet the B3408 at Wherwell.

The route turns right here C signposted Longparish, but you might like to make a detour to visit Wherwell. This village is one of Hampshire's most charming and was the site of a priory in Saxon days. **If so, turn left, and then left again by the cenotaph, towards the church to a car park on the left. Return to C.**

A beautiful road now follows the west bank of the River Test, shadowed by the trees of Harewood Forest. **In 2 miles you approach the A303. Just before the A303, turn left still following the B3048 signposted Longparish.**

67

Farley Mount Country Park, near Winchester
The whole area is a Site of Special Scientific Interest noted for its rare orchids. Settled by man from earliest times, it is dotted with prehistoric burial mounds. In the West Wood, the remains of a Roman villa with a fine mosaic floor have been excavated. A burial mound at the western end of the park is crowned by a pyramid in memory of a horse which saved its owner from falling into a quarry. The horse was renamed 'Beware Chalk Pit'.

From Beacon Hill pleasant short walks lead to Farley Chamberlayne Church and to the hamlet of Ashley.

Open at all times. Telephone: Winchester (01962) 846034

Highclere Castle
The castle was designed by Sir Charles Barry, builder of the Houses of Parliament, and the grounds were laid out by 'Capability' Brown.

Open July, August and September, Wednesday–Sunday and Bank Holidays. Grounds 12–6. House 1–6. Telephone: Newbury (01635) 253210

Sandham Memorial Chapel, Burghclere
In 1927 Stanley Spencer was commissioned by the Behrends family of Burghclere to paint the murals, and they took him ten years to complete. There is no violence in the paintings. The hospital scenes show the nursing orderlies and the wounded attempting to live as normal a life as possible under desperately difficult conditions. Most impressive is the resurrection scene on the central wall. The soldiers are seen rising from their graves, each carrying his cross to lay at the feet of Jesus.

Open 25 March–end October, Wednesday–Sunday and Bank Holidays, 11.30–6. November and March, Saturday and Sunday only, 11.30–4. Telephone: Newbury (01635) 278394

Follow the road as it bears right to bridge the A303 and continue to a junction. Turn left for Longparish still following the B3048. As its name suggests, Longparish has an exceptionally long main street. It is lined with attractive cottages, many thatched and half-timbered with warm red brick infilling. **Continue on the B3048 for Hurstbourne Priors.** Approaching the village, the little River Bourne flows into the River Test and the route now follows the course of the stream to the 'Hampshire Highlands'.

In Hurstbourne Priors the road runs to an off-set crossroads. Bear right for

a few yards and then left to resume the route along the B3048 signposted St Mary Bourne. St Mary Bourne is another enchanting village of brick and flint thatched cottages. The twelfth-century church has a black Tournai marble font, chained bible and splendid effigy of a Crusader.

Keep to the main road as it runs through Stoke to Hurstbourne Tarrant. This village, beloved by William Cobbett, rivals St Mary Bourne for beauty. Streamside cottages, set in gently curving meadows, are linked to the road by tiny bridges. Beyond the village rise steep hillsides of elm, oak and ash, the

famous 'hangers' of Hampshire. Jane Austen often walked here to visit her friends, the Debaries, who lived at the rectory. She delighted in this lovely scenery which she believed must be 'one of the joys of heaven'. She stayed with her friends, the Lloyds, at Ibthorpe which is the next village on the route.

Just past the Plough Inn, the road meets the A343. Turn right for a few yards and then left signposted Upton and Vernham Dean D. The sign is not clearly angled so look for a sign for Ibthorpe at the bottom of the wall on the left as you turn. After ¼ mile, eighteenth-century Ibthorpe House, where Jane Austen stayed, is on the right beyond a small green with a wooden bench. **Follow the road to a junction in Upton. Keep ahead signposted Vernham Dean.**

At the crossroads in Vernham Dean turn right along Bulpitts Hill signposted Vernham Street and Linkenholt. Keep to the main road as it climbs the downs and bears left for Vernham Street. Continue past the turning on the left for Littledown and look care-

A horse's memorial in Farley Mount Country Park

St Mary Bourne, one of the lovely villages in the Bourne valley

fully for a road on the right signposted Linkenholt. **Turn right as directed and continue for about a mile past the church in Linkenholt to a T-junction. Turn left signposted Faccombe.** As the road curves round Cleve Hill there are spectacular views. **At the T-junction turn right signposted Netherton. In Netherton village turn left signposted Faccombe. When the road divides, keep ahead (right-hand road) past the Jack Russell Inn. A track joins on the left but keep ahead (right-hand road) to a T-junction. Turn right for a few yards and then turn left signposted Ashmansworth and Highclere. At the T-junction in Ashmansworth turn left signposted Newbury.** The road runs high over the downs to cross the ancient line of the Ox Drove and meet the A343. **Turn left signposted Highclere. Follow the A343 for about 2 miles and then at the crossroads turn right signposted Penwood and Burghclere.** The road runs through woodlands for 1½ miles and bridges the A34. **Immediately after the bridge there is a T-junction ⧆. Turn right following the brown sign for Highclere Castle.** More signs direct you to the

castle entrance. The castle is the home of the Earl and Countess of Carnarvon and is an example of Victorian Gothic-style architecture at its most impressive.

Return to ⧆ and keep straight ahead signposted Burghclere. Bear right at the next junction and, after a few yards, look for the sign for the Sandham Memorial Chapel on the right where there is off-road parking. The chapel is a unique war memorial. The walls are covered with magnificent murals painted by Stanley Spencer depicting his experiences as a medical orderly during the First World War.

Just past the chapel turn right down Spring Lane signposted Ecchinswell and Kingsclere. When you meet the T-junction turn right, still for Ecchinswell and Kingsclere. Pass the turning to Ecchinswell and continue along the right-hand road for Sydmonton. The road runs south towards the slopes of Watership Down, the setting for Richard Adams' novel. **At the T-junction turn left signposted Kingsclere ⧆. In a little more than 3 miles the road divides south of Kingsclere. Bear right to meet the B3051 and then bear right again signposted Overton.** There are

beautiful downland views as the road climbs White Hill to the top of Stubbington Down. There is a car park and picnic place here and footpaths follow the crest of Watership Down. **At the Y-junction keep to the B3051 signposted Overton.**

Approaching Overton, drive past the church to meet the B3400 at a crossroads. Continue straight over, signposted Micheldever, and drive through Overton. This is an attractive market town with many old houses set back from the road. **Keep to the main road as it bears a little left signposted Micheldever. Continue south to cross the railway and go under the A303 signposted Micheldever Station. Go over the crossroads, past Micheldever Station on the right, and keep ahead for Micheldever village.** Once a royal town owned by King Alfred, today Micheldever is a pleasant village with many old thatched houses and a working smithy. **Pass the church on the right to a T-junction. Turn right signposted Stoke Charity to follow the south bank of the River Dever.** Shaded by tall trees in a gentle river valley, Stoke Charity must be Hampshire at its most retiring!

Follow the road through the village and bear left signposted Sutton Scotney. Continue along the valley through Wonston to Sutton Scotney. Drive past a road on the left to a T-junction and turn right. Continue for about 50 yards (46 metres) and then turn left along the A30 signed Salisbury. The road bridges the A34. **After 1½ miles turn left along the A272 signposted Winchester. At the roundabout bear right, still following the B3420 for Winchester. In the town follow the signs for the station, over the crossroads, turning right and right again for the station entrance.** ▪

A WRITER'S HAMPSHIRE: JANE AUSTEN, GILBERT WHITE AND CHARLES KINGSLEY

60 MILES – 3½ HOURS
START AND FINISH AT OVERTON

The life of the north Hampshire countryside is at the heart of Jane Austen's novels, and this tour visits Steventon, where she wrote her early work, and Chawton Cottage (now called Jane Austen's House) where she completed her later novels. Gilbert White captured the quiet beauty of the county in his History of Selborne, *and the River Itchen flowing through its lush watermeadows inspired Charles Kingsley to write* The Water Babies. *But there is more than literary interest in this tour. It includes visits to stately homes, Hinton Ampner and Avington House, and offers an opportunity of a trip on the Mid-Hants Steam Railway, the Watercress Line.*

Overton is a large village in the valley of the River Test, 8 miles west of Basingstoke. **Leave Overton heading east along the B3400 signed Basingstoke. Pass a turning to Ashe.** The pleasant undulating countryside around this village has changed little since Jane Austen walked here to visit her friends, the Lefroys, at Ashe House. **Continue for a further mile then turn right past the Deane Gate pub signposted Steventon. Follow the lane to Steventon under the railway, then turn left signposted Steventon Church Ⓐ. After ¼ mile turn right up Church Lane signposted Steventon Church.** The rectory where Jane Austen was born stood on the corner. It was a well-built, two-storeyed house with a trellised porch and a front door opening straight into the parlour. All that remains are some railings which, before it was stolen, surrounded an iron water-pump. The iron pump replaced a wooden one that once served the Austen family. But the simple twelfth-century church where she worshipped stands on the left at the top of Church Lane. There is room to park here.

Retrace the route down Church Lane, turning left to the T-junction at Ⓐ. Turn left signposted Micheldever Station to run to a cross-roads. Turn left signposted North Waltham and, in a little more than a mile, just past the church in the village, follow the road signposted Dummer and Basingstoke. The road meets the A30 by the Wheatsheaf Inn. Jane Austen often walked to the inn from Steventon to collect the mail. **Turn left for a few yards along the A30 and then turn right, signposted Axford, to drive under the motorway. Continue for ½ mile then turn left for Dummer Ⓑ. At the T-junction turn right signposted Farleigh Wallop and drive past the pond.**

Chawton Cottage, Jane Austen's home from 1809 until her death in 1817

· PLACES OF INTEREST ·

Overton

Overton lies close to the source of the River Test. It is a large village with a wide main street lined with attractive houses. In the past it was an important staging post on the coach route from London to Exeter. Yearly sheep fairs were held in Winchester Street. After the First World War, Portals, the company which produces bank-note paper for world markets, moved here from Laverstoke.

Jane Austen at Steventon and Chawton

Jane Austen was born in 1775, the seventh of the Austens' eight children. Lively and attractive, she enjoyed dancing and parties and had many friends in the neighbourhood. Her father, the Reverend George Austen, had an extensive library and Jane read widely. Growing up within the

circle of a happy, loving family she was able to develop the personal

qualities which give her books their moral integrity and improve and polish her own natural gifts as a writer. From an early age she was writing witty stories and sketches to amuse her family and, by the age of twenty-five, she had completed three novels which she

was to revise extensively before publication. In 1801 Jane moved with her parents to Bath, but it was not until she was able to resume a settled life in the country at Chawton in 1809 that she began writing once more. *Sense and Sensibility* was published in 1811 followed by *Pride and Prejudice* in 1813, *Mansfield Park* in 1814 and *Emma* in 1815. Jane died in 1817. *Northanger Abbey* and *Persuasion* were published after her death. It is sad that so fine a novelist should die so young, but she has secured her place as one of England's greatest writers.

Jane Austen's House is open April–October, daily. November, December and March, Wednesday–Sunday. January and February, Saturday and Sunday. 11–4.30. Telephone: Selborne (01420) 83262

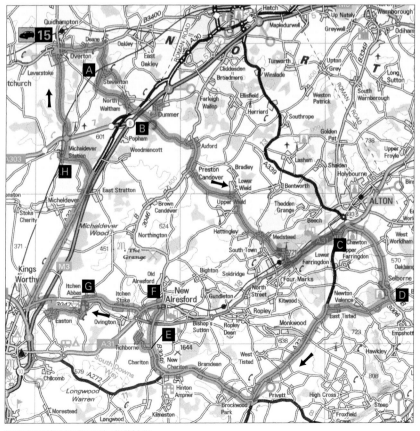

SCALE 1:250 000 OR 1 INCH TO 4 MILES *1 CM TO 2.5 KM*

The Wakes, Gilbert White's house in Selborne

Dummer Church is on the right. Mainly twelfth century, it has a seventeenth-century gallery and a rare medieval rood canopy.

Retrace the route to the T-junction at ▣ **and turn left signposted Axford and the Candovers. Continue to meet the B3046 at Axford. Turn right signposted Alresford and the Candovers and continue along the B3046 to Preston Candover. Pass the pub and, just before the church, turn left signposted Wield.** The road runs south-east over rolling chalk downlands. **When the road divides keep ahead signposted Lower Wield. Pass the turning on the left to Lower Wield and continue to a T-junction. Turn right, signposted Medstead, for only about 100 yards (91 metres) and then turn left, signposted Medstead. At the T-junction in Medstead turn left, signposted Medstead, for a few yards and then right to pass the church on the left. Keep straight ahead over the crossroads signposted Four Marks and Ropley to an awkward junction of three roads. Turn left for a few yards and then right down Roe Downs Road. At the T-junction turn left signposted Four Marks and Alton. The road turns right and on the corner there is a car park and picnic area at the approach to Chawton Park Woods.** Footpaths lead through the woods where Jane Austen once walked.

They were part of the Chawton House Estate inherited by one of her brothers, Edward.

Turn left from the car park and follow the road as it bears right to meet the A31. Turn left signposted Alton and Chawton. This road is the old royal highway from Winchester to London. Known as 'The Pass of Alton', it once provided rich pickings for highwaymen. **Follow the A31 for about 3 miles. At the roundabout leave the main road and take the road on the right signposted Chawton** ▣**. The road bears left. Jane Austen's House is signed on the left and the car park for the house is on your right behind the car park for the pub.** Cross the road to visit the homely cottage surrounded by a pretty garden where Jane Austen wrote her masterpieces. It has been preserved very much as it was in her time.

To continue the tour leave Jane Austen's House on your left and drive through Chawton, bearing right to meet the B3006. Turn right signposted Selborne and Gilbert White's House. Continue for 4 miles to drive into Selborne. A car park is signed on the right behind the Selborne Arms. Across the village street from the church and the rectory is The Wakes, the home of Gilbert White from the age of ten until his death at seventy-two. His delightful *History of Selborne* reflects the close study he made of the surrounding countryside

and the pleasure he took in all aspects of its wildlife. His grave is in the churchyard.

Continue south through Selborne and then leave the B3006 and turn right signposted Newton Valence ▣**. Keep straight on for about 3½ miles past the turning to Newton Valence to meet the A32 at East Tisted. Turn left signposted West Meon and continue along the A32 for 6 miles to its junction with the A272 at the West Meon Hut (restaurant). Turn right signposted Winchester.** After 1½ miles you pass a leafy lane on the left leading to Brockwood Park. During the nineteenth century this was the home of Colonel Greenwood who wrote a book describing a method of transplanting fully grown trees, *The Tree Lifter*. The beautiful copper beeches you see lining the road were probably planted under his supervision. **Continue through Bramdean.** The road running through the village was widened in 1943 to facilitate the passage of military vehicles prior to the D-Day landings. **Continue following the signs for Hinton Ampner Gardens and turn left as directed if you wish to visit them. Turn left from the entrance to the gardens to continue along the A272.**

Turn right at the crossroads in New Cheriton along the B3046 signposted Cheriton and New Alresford. Keep to the main road signposted Alresford through Cheriton. It is hard to imagine that this attractive village threaded by the River Itchen was once a battlefield. The battle of Cheriton, fought in 1644 and won by Parliament troops, proved a turning point in the Civil War. **Continue along the B3046 and turn left for Tichborne** ▣**. Follow the lane over the River Itchen to the village. Look carefully for a lane on the left signposted to the church and drive up to**

Gilbert White at Selborne

Gilbert White was born in the vicarage at Selborne and lived at The Wakes from 1731 until his death in 1793. Unmarried, he lived a comfortable life in beautiful surroundings. Most of his time was spent studying the natural world.

The Wakes was purchased in 1950 as a memorial to his achievements, the funds being largely provided by the Oates family. There are displays about Captain Lawrence Oates, one of the heroes of Scott's ill-fated 1911 Antarctic Expedition. Leaflets in the house give details of walks around the village, Selborne Common, and through the beech woods of Selborne's famous 'Hanger'.

The house is open end April–October, daily, 11–5. Winter, weekends only. Telephone: Selborne (01420) 511275

Hinton Ampner

Hinton Ampner House is charming and contains a fascinating collection of furniture and paintings. The gardens are some of the finest in Hampshire.

The house is open April–end September. August, Tuesday, Wednesday and weekends. 1.30–5.30. Garden open weekends, Tuesday and Wednesday, 1.30–5.30. Telephone: Alresford (01962) 771305

Tichborne

The origins of the Tichborne Dole date from the twelfth century. On her deathbed Lady Mabella begged her husband to give the value of a small part of their land to the poor. He offered her as much land as she could crawl round carrying a burning brand. She encircled 23 acres, now known as 'The Crawls'. Each Lady Day, 25 March,

the villagers gather at Tichborne House to collect their 'Dole' – 7lbs flour for each adult and half as much for each child.

Mid-Hants Steam Railway

This historic steam railway runs over ten miles between Alresford and Alton. There are two intermediate stations at Medstead and Ropley. Telephone: Alresford (01962) 733810. Talking timetable: (01962) 733810

Avington House and Park, Near Itchen Abbas

The house was rebuilt at the time of Charles II who found it a convenient home for Nell Gwynne! Park open all times. House open May–September, Sunday and Bank Holidays, 2–5.30. Telephone: Alresford (01962) 779260

---

the parking area. Tichborne Church must not be missed. It has its original door with an iron sanctuary ring, a Saxon chancel with splayed windows and carved Jacobean pews like small rooms. From the church there is a lovely view of this charming village of thatched houses dotted about in meadows framed by wooded hillsides.

Retrace the route from the church down the lane, turning right to rejoin the B3046 at **E**. Turn left and follow the signs for New Alresford over the A31, through the town and under the railway bridge to meet the B3047 **F**.

For a trip on the Mid-Hants Steam Railway turn right signed Alton and follow the signs right for the station. Return to **F** and continue ahead signed Winchester.

If you do not visit the railway, turn left at **F** signed Winchester. Continue for about a mile and then turn right, still on the B3047, signposted King's Worthy. The road runs along the Itchen valley through Itchen Stoke to Itchen Abbas. Charles Kingsley stayed at an earlier Plough Inn, and the sparkling water of the River Itchen, which he described as 'the loveliest of

vale rivers', inspired *The Water Babies*. **Just past the Plough Inn turn left signposted Avington Park **G** to cross the river to a T-junction. Turn right past the church and the entrance to Avington House. Turn right signposted Easton and Winchester. Follow the lane through Avington Park beside the river to Easton.** The park is open for walks and picnics and there are parking areas beside the road. **The road bends left in Easton and then right to a T-junction. Turn right to recross the River Itchen and meet the B3047. Turn left signposted King's Worthy and Winchester to drive through Abbots Worthy and meet the A33. Turn right signposted Basingstoke. Continue north for about 8 miles past two turnings for Micheldever. Turn left signposted Micheldever Station. After 1½ miles, just before the railway bridge, turn right at the crossroads signposted Overton **H**. Follow the signs for 5 miles back to Overton.** ■

Itchen Abbas, a charming riverside village

THE ALICE HOLT FOREST AND BASING HOUSE

45 MILES – 3 HOURS
START AND FINISH AT ALTON

The special appeal of rural Hampshire with its gentle hills, ancient forests and old-world villages can be enjoyed to the full on this tour. It includes a visit to the ruins of Basing House and offers opportunities for a boat trip along a restored section of the Basingstoke Canal and a ride on the Mid-Hants Steam Railway. Two delightful country towns, Alton and Odiham, can also be explored.

With the main entrance to the railway station on your left leave Alton heading south-east along Paper Mill Lane (B3004) signposted Bordon. The road runs under the A31 then takes a more easterly course to East Worldham. Turn left up the lane sign-posted to the church where there is a parking area. Philippa Chaucer, the wife of the poet Geoffrey Chaucer, is buried in the church. **Return** down the lane and turn left to continue along the B3004 to the top of an escarpment. A marvellous view opens up ahead over wooded countryside to the Surrey hills. Geoffrey Chaucer's son, Thomas, was keeper of the Royal Forest of Woolmer. The patches of open sandy heath and scattered woodlands immediately ahead are remnants of this once great forest, the haunt of wild boar and red deer. As you descend the slope, the hill on the right is called after that keen huntsman, King John.

Keep ahead through Kingsley to meet the A325. Turn left signposted Farnham to follow the A325 as it runs north to enter the Alice Holt Woodland Park (part of the Alice Holt Forest).

Continue for 2 miles to Bucks Horn Oak in the heart of the forest. Turn right in front of The Halfway House pub, following the sign for the Forest Visitor Centre. Turn left following the signs to car parks and a landscaped picnic area beside a lake. The Visitor Centre has a shop

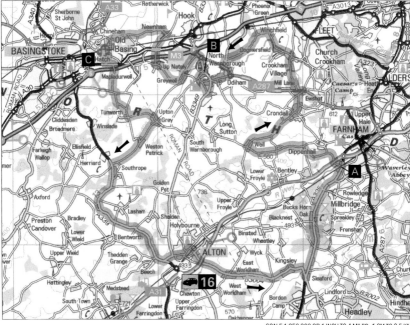

SCALE 1:250 000 OR 1 INCH TO 4 MILES 1 CM TO 2.5 KM

Leafy glades in the Alice Holt Woodland Park

and provides all the information you need to follow waymarked trails on foot or bike (bikes can be hired), including an easy-access trail for wheelchairs and families with young children.

A wide variety of wildlife includes roe deer and the spectacular Purple Emperor butterfly.

From the Visitor Centre car park retrace the route to the A325, turning right from the entrance and right again in front of the Halfway House. Turn right onto the A325. After a mile the entrance to Birdworld will be passed on the left.

• PLACES OF INTEREST •

Alton

Alton is an attractive town with a wealth of old inns proving its importance as a market and

former coaching centre. During the Civil War the Cavaliers in Alton were surprised by a party of Roundheads. After fighting their way through the town the Cavaliers, led by Colonel Boles, held out in the church. Colonel Boles was killed as he made his last stand in the pulpit. The church door is heavily pock-marked with bullet holes, and the remains of lead bullets are embedded in the columns of the Norman tower. The pillars of the tower are decorated with amusing carvings of animals and birds, among them a wolf gnawing a bone and two donkeys with their heels in the air. Fifteenth-century wall paintings can be seen on the north face of one of the pillars.

The town is surrounded by some of the loveliest countryside in Hampshire, and in summer the fields are green with the hops grown for Alton's breweries.

The Curtis Museum in the High Street has a display on hops and brewing, many interesting archaeological finds and a collection of children's toys.

Open Tuesday–Saturday, 10–5. Telephone: Alton (01420) 82802

Alice Holt Woodland Park

Alice Holt, like Woolmer, was formerly a royal hunting forest, and is now carefully managed for the benefit of its visitors and its wildlife. Unlike Woolmer, the soil is a rich loam supporting fine oak trees. In times past they provided timber for England's navy, and are still harvested today. Alice Holt oak is being used to build a replica of Shakespeare's Globe Theatre in London. The Forest Visitor Centre and shop is open Wednesday––Sunday, 9–4.45. Telephone: Alton (01420) 23666

Birdworld

Spectacular birds can be seen in gardens and parkland and there is a special children's farm. Picnic sites, a café and gift shop. Open daily from 9.30. Telephone: (01420) 22140

Basingstoke Canal

The canal was completed in 1794 to transport timber and agricultural produce from the market town of Basingstoke, via the Wey navigation and the River Thames, to London. After falling into disuse, restoration work began in 1973 and, today, it provides a beautiful and peaceful waterway with over 30 miles of towpath available as a permissive footpath. The canal is exceptionally rich in plants and dragonflies.

Odiham

The High Street of this old town is a happy mix of half-timbered Tudor cottages and Georgian houses. The impressive church stands among cottages beside the River Bury. It is mainly fourteenth century and has several fine brasses some of which date from the fifteenth century. North of the churchyard are the old stocks and whipping post.

A short walk from the High Street, at Colt Hill, is a car park for the Basingstoke Canal, a good starting point for local walks or boat trips. The narrow boat *John Pinkerton* offers trips of 2¹/₂ hours on the canal from April to June.

Odiham Castle can be visited at all times.

Basing House, Old Basing

The huge Tudor palace built by Sir William Paulet, 1st Marquess of Winchester, covered 8 acres and was looted and burnt by Cromwell's soldiers after a siege lasting two years. Today, the site, with its dovecote towers, secret tunnel, restored garden and spectacular barn, still conveys a good impression of the once magnificent mansion.

There is an exhibition telling the story of the epic siege, and the events are frequently re-enacted. The site is open April– September, Wednesday–Sunday and Bank Holidays, 2–6. Telephone: Basingstoke (01256) 467294

Mid-Hants Steam Railway

The restored line runs for 10 miles between Alton and Alresford. There are two intermediate stations at Medstead and Ropley where a variety of steam locomotives can be seen undergoing restoration. Days in steam vary so for details ring Alresford (01962) 733810. Talking timetable: (01962) 733810

Continue along the A325 in the direction of Farnham through Holt Pound. After about 1¹/₂ miles leave the A325 and turn left at the traffic lights, just before a railway bridge A. There is no signpost so be careful not to miss this turn! The road runs under another railway bridge and crosses the River Wey to meet the A31. Drive straight across taking the road ahead signposted Dippenhall. Continue for about ¹/₂ mile then turn right downhill signposted Dippenhall. At the T-junction turn left to run to another T-junction. Turn left signposted Well and Long Sutton. The road crosses a ridge of high fertile country dotted with

historic remains including an Iron Age castle and the site of a Roman villa.

Little can be seen from the road but, after about a mile, if you stop in a parking area in front of a gate on the right, you can follow a footpath for about 100 yards (91 metres) to a small wood, the site of Barley Pound. At one time this was the hiding place of an outlaw, Adam de Gurdon.

In 2 miles the road leads to the tiny hamlet of Well. Turn right signposted Crondall. On the left, as you might expect, is a fine well. A plaque states that it was a gift to the villagers from William Fullerton who died at Well Manor in 1888. **Follow the signs for Crondall.** The route takes you through pleasantly varied

countryside of woods, farms and downs with wide views.

Drive into Crondall village and turn right up the first lane on the right just before the Plume of Feathers Inn. At the top of the lane there is a parking area in front of the church. There is much to enjoy inside the magnificent Norman church. On the chancel floor is the famous brass of a fourteenth-century rector, Nicholas de Caerwent. **Retrace the route and turn right to continue through the village for Crookham. At the T-junction turn right to meet the A287. Turn left along the A287 for about 100 yards (91 metres) and then turn right signposted Crookham Village.** The road runs through woods and in just over a mile crosses the Basingstoke Canal. Immediately after the bridge there is a tree-shaded car park and picnic area beside the canal on the left.

Drive into Crookham Village and at the T-junction turn left signposted Dogmersfield. Keep to the main road for Dogmersfield and continue as it bears right then left through the village to run close to the Basingstoke Canal. Opposite the Barley Mow pub there is another large car park on the left by the canal. **Continue along the main road to a cross-roads. Turn left signposted Winchfield Station. In about ¹/₂ mile turn left signposted Winchfield Church and Odiham. The road runs for 2¹/₂ miles through the woods of Odiham Common to meet the B3016. Turn left signposted Odiham and continue to meet the A287. Turn left for Odiham to a roundabout and bear right signed for Odiham. Drive along the main street of this charming old market town.** The historic buildings are best explored on foot. Several car parks are signed on the left and right of the road.

Odiham Castle, from here King John rode to sign the Magna Carta

Continue through Odiham to meet the B3349. Turn left signposted Alton. Take the next road on the right signposted Greywell to drive over the top of Odiham Firs. This high point was the site of a beacon used as a signalling post to warn of possible invasion by the Armada.

Turn left at the T-junction and continue to another T-junction. Turn right here to drive through part of North Warnborough. Be careful not to miss the next turn! About 100 yards (91 metres) after passing the Anchor pub on the left turn left **B** to follow the lane to parking areas beside a lifting bridge over the Basingstoke Canal. This is a delightful spot with seats by the waterside. If you cross the bridge and turn left to follow the towpath for about ¼ mile you will see the remains of Odiham Castle. It has a thirteenth-century octagonal keep, the only one of this shape in England. In 1215 King John set out from the castle to sign the Magna Carta.

Retrace the route down the lane to **B** and turn left along the B3349. Keep straight on at the first roundabout signed Hook. Before the motorway (M3), turn left signposted Greywell. There is a car park on the right giving access to footpaths on Bartley Heath and North Warnborough Green. Approaching Greywell village you pass the entrance to the Greywell Tunnel on the Basingstoke Canal, the largest bat roost in Britain. Continue through Greywell, a most attractive village of thatched half-timbered houses. The road curves north-west from Greywell to the village of Up Nately. Pass the church and turn right signposted Newnham to cross the Basingstoke Canal and the motorway. Continue for ½ mile to meet the A30. Drive across and take the road ahead signposted Newnham.

At the crossroads in Newnham village turn left signposted Basing. Keep to the main road as it runs west for 3½ miles through meadows and woods and descends into the Lodden valley to a T-junction. Turn left signposted Old Basing. On the corner is the site of Oliver's Battery where Cromwell's Parliamentary troops stationed their guns during the siege of Basing House. Keep to the main road as it bears right through Old Basing village. Just past the church one of the entrances to the ruins of Basing House is on the left, but you need to follow a rather convoluted route to reach the car park. Follow the signs to the car park and do not give up hope! The ruins of Basing House are one of Hampshire's most fascinating treasures.

Retrace the route, turning left at the car park entrance, left at the next junction and then left again. Turn right just past the Crown Inn up Crown Lane. At the traffic lights there is a junction of several roads. Do not take the first road on the right but turn right down the second, Byfleet Avenue **C**. Cross the A30 and bridge the motorway to follow the road to a T-junction at Polecat Corner. Turn left signposted Tunworth and Upton Grey and after a few yards turn right following the same signs. Now follow the signs for Upton Grey. This is one of the prettiest villages in Hampshire, graced with seventeenth-century houses.

Just past the pond in Upton Grey, at the crossroads, turn right signposted Weston Patrick. Follow the road through Weston Patrick to meet the A339. Turn left to follow the A339 back to Alton.

The extensive ruins of Basing House, Old Basing

STRATFIELD SAYE, SILCHESTER ROMAN TOWN AND THE VYNE

49 MILES – 3 HOURS
START AND FINISH AT HOOK

Highlights of this short, but fascinating, tour in north-east Hampshire are visits to Stratfield Saye, the gift of a grateful nation to the Duke of Wellington in 1817; The Vyne, a National Trust property set in beautiful grounds threaded by the River Loddon; and a circuit of Calleva Atrebatum *at Silchester, the best preserved Roman town in Britain. Along the way there are opportunities to explore attractive villages and walk and picnic in forests and country parks.*

This is a rather complex tour so please navigate carefully.

Hook is situated beside the A30 about 5 miles east of Basingstoke. **From Hook head east along the A30 signed Hartley Wintney. Keep straight on over the crossroads at Phoenix Green following the signs for Hartley Wintney.** Although the countryside is only

The Wellington memorial surmounted by a statue of the 'Iron Duke'

semi-rural in appearance the houses are set in attractive surroundings of heath, commons and small woods. **Keep to the main road (A30) through Hartley Wintney to cross the River Hart at Hartfordbridge and enter beautiful mixed woodland. After about 1/2 mile turn left signposted Reading, Finchampstead and Eversley. Drive through the woods to a T-junction and turn left, A327, signposted Eversley. Keep straight on for about 11/2 miles. Look carefully for a lane on the left signposted Eversley Church. Turn left as directed and park a few yards down the lane by the church on the right.** Charles Kingsley, whose books advocating social reforms include *The Water Babies*, was rector here from 1842 to 1875. Inside the church a beautiful window in the chancel commemorates the centenary of his arrival at Eversley. It shows St Elizabeth of Hungary (the subject of his poem *The Saint's Tragedy*) with a Water Baby either side of her.

Kingsley's grave is in the church-yard. If you walk a little further down the lane you will see the gracious Elizabethan rectory (with later additions) which was Kingsley's home.

Return to the main road, turn left, and head north for just over 1/4 mile to a crossroads A. Turn left signposted Bramshill and Heckfield. Continue through more pleasantly wooded countryside past Bramshill. The road crosses the River Whitewater and, in 1/2 mile, meets the B3011. Turn right along the B3011 signposted Reading. The road runs through the woods for 1/2 mile to meet the B3349. Turn right at the roundabout following the signs for the Wellington Country Park. In just over a mile, at the roundabout, turn right to follow the signs into the park where there are large car parks on the right. Woods and meadows surround a large lake and this is the perfect place to relax, walk, picnic or, perhaps,

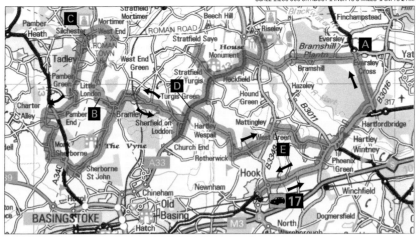

hire a boat or canoe. There are waymarked nature trails and in the deer park red, roe and fallow deer can be seen.

To continue the tour drive out of the park entrance to the roundabout and turn left along the B3349 signposted Hook and Fleet. Brown signs indicate the way to Stratfield Saye House. **At the next roundabout turn right following the signs for Stratfield Saye House.**

Ahead you will see the monument erected in memory of the Duke of Wellington, a tall column surmounted by a statue. **The road meets the A33 in front of the monument. Turn left following the signs to the house and continue for about 2 miles. Turn right following the signs by the Wellington Arms Hotel. Keep following the signs over the river to turn right at a T-junction.**

The entrance to Stratfield Saye House is through the lodge gates on the right. This 200-year-old house is surprisingly unostentatious, reflecting throughout the taste of Wellington who disliked grandeur and unnecessary expense. The present Duke has preserved the house as a family home. Although the tour is restricted to the ground floor you will enjoy a unique collection of furniture and pictures.

Retrace the route to the junction with the A33 at the Wellington Arms Hotel. Turn right along the A33 signposted Basingstoke. Cross the River Loddon by Longbridge Mill, said to be haunted by a ghost rattling chains in the approved fashion. After crossing the river continue and then turn right to follow the road for Bramley through the attractive village of Sherfield on Loddon. At the junction keep ahead for Bramley to cross a small stream. A circle of dense woodland on the left encloses the embankments of a triple-ringed Iron Age fort.

Follow the road into Bramley, continuing over the railway through this long village. There are many charming brick cottages with small leaded windows and tile-hung first storeys. **Turn right**

• PLACES OF INTEREST •

Wellington Country Park
The park is ideal for family visits as there is something to please everyone. Children are well provided for with a small farm, an adventure playground and a miniature steam railway. They may also enjoy the Thames Valley Time Trail which uses life-size models to illustrate history from the time of the dinosaurs. An unusual feature is the National Dairy Museum. Special events are staged in summer in the Waterloo Meadow.
Restaurant and tearoom. Park open March–October, daily. Winter, weekends, 10–4 or 5.30 depending on time of dusk. Telephone: Reading (01734) 26444

Stratfield Saye
Stratfield Saye was built about 1630 by Sir William Pitt and, apart

from the outer gabled wings, it still preserves the character of a Jacobean house. In Georgian times sash windows were substituted for the original mullions, and the small entrance porch was added in 1838.
The library was the Duke's favourite room and has changed little since his day. The adjoining Music Room is dedicated to the memory of Copenhagen, the horse who bore him throughout the battle of Waterloo and whose grave is in the grounds.
The wonderful Dutch and Flemish paintings in the Drawing Room came from the captured baggage-train of Joseph Bonaparte after his defeat at the battle of Vittoria in 1813.
Refreshments. Open May–last Sunday in September, Saturday–Thursday, 11.30–4. Basingstoke (01256) 882882

Silchester Roman Town

Before the coming of the Romans this was the site of a great Celtic fort. Gradually it developed into a town built on the Roman plan and became known as *Calleva Atrebatum*, the capital of the Atrebates, a Celtic tribe. The remains of the walls which surrounded the town and followed the line of the Celtic embankments can still be seen. They were originally 10 feet (3 metres) thick and up to 25 feet (8 metres) high enclosing an area of around 100 acres and pierced in four places by strong gates. In the centre was the forum surrounded by the public buildings and shops. The remains of three temples, some baths and houses and a large basilica have all been excavated. But the most exciting find was the discovery of the remains of a tiny Christian church, dating from the fourth century. At present it is the only church known to have been built during the Roman occupation.

Although the site is now grassed over and farmed, the story of the town is told in the site museum in Silchester village, from where a track leads to a footpath which crosses the site to St Mary's Church.

The museum and site are open throughout the year during daylight hours. Telephone: Reading (01734) 700362

The Vyne

Among many impressive features are a remarkable oak gallery, a splendid sweeping staircase and an exquisite early sixteenth-century chapel described by Horace Walpole as the 'most heavenly chapel in the world'.

National Trust shop and tearooms. Open 25 March–end September, Tuesday–Thursday and weekends, 1.30–5.30. Telephone: Basingstoke (01256) 881337

---

following the sign to the **Parish Church where there is parking.** The church, dating from the twelfth century, has walls 3 feet (1 metre) thick built from flints, tiles and Roman red brick brought from the nearby Roman city of *Calleva Atrebatum*, near Silchester. Inside there are fine medieval wall paintings and early stained-glass windows, including a lovely window of Flemish sixteenth-century glass saved from destruction by Cromwell's forces by being concealed in the moat of Beaurepaire House, a mile south of the village.

From the church, return to the road and turn right to continue for about ³/₄ mile to a T-junction **B**. **Turn right signposted Latchmere Green and Silchester to follow the** line of the old Roman road. **Pass Frog Lane on the left and continue to another T-junction. Turn right for just a few yards and then turn left signposted Church.** Shortly, on the left, is the thrilling sight of the remains of the white walls of *Calleva Atrebatum*. Dating from the third century AD, they are built of coursed flint with stone bonding held together with lime mortar, and still encircle the grassed-over site of the city, rising in places to over 20 feet (6 metres) in height. There is parking by the small Church of St Mary on the left which contains a delicately-carved fifteenth-century chancel screen. From the church a footpath leads over the site to the museum in Silchester, a distance of about a mile. (The museum can be visited by car later in the tour.)

Continue along Wall Lane as it curves left past the remains of the Roman amphitheatre on the right. At the T-junction turn left signposted Silchester and Tadley. Continue for about ¹/₂ mile and then turn left signposted Little London and Silchester. After a few yards the road forks **C**.

To see the museum, take the left-hand road and follow the signs.

To continue the tour, bear right at the fork signposted Little London and Basingstoke. The road runs south through Silchester village and part of ancient Pamber Forest. **Drive through Little London to a T-junction. Turn right signposted Basingstoke and continue to meet the A340. Turn right signposted Tadley for just a few yards and then turn left signposted Charter Alley to a T-junction. Follow the main road bearing left signed Charter Alley and Ramsdell.** In about ¹/₄ mile, a splendid oak avenue leads to Pamber Priory Church. A Benedictine abbey was founded here in the twelfth century, and the church incorporates the remains of the priory which

Stratfield Saye, the gift of a grateful nation to the Duke of Wellington

The Vyne, one of Hampshire's most beautiful and historic houses

was attached to the abbey, notably the central tower and exquisite thirteenth-century choir.

Continue for Monk Sherborne past a road on the right. At the T-junction turn right signposted Monk Sherborne. Keep on for Sherborne St John past the pub in Monk Sherborne. Continue along the main road as it bears left in the direction of Sherborne St John. In a mile the road meets the A340. Turn right signposted Basing-stoke for just a few yards then leave the A340 and turn left signposted Sherborne St John to enter this pretty village. At the T-junction turn left signposted Bramley and Sherfield on Loddon. Follow the main road as it bends

right signposted Bramley before curving north. After about 1 1/4 miles the entrance to a fine stately home, The Vyne, is on the left. A visit to this mellow Tudor House, to which many additions have been made through the centuries, is a 'must'.

With the entrance to The Vyne on your left continue the tour to a T-junction in Bramley. For the next 4 miles the tour retraces part of the earlier route. Turn right to follow the road over the rail-way, through Bramley Green and Sherfield on Loddon to meet the A33. Turn left along the A33 signposted Reading. Cross the River Lyde and in 1/2 mile leave the main road and turn right sign-posted Hartley Wespall and

Rotherwick **D**. Keep straight on through tranquil wooded countryside before following the road as it turns right into the village of Lyde Green. Keep ahead for about 3/4 mile and then turn left signposted Mattingley to run past the pond in Rotherwick. Keep ahead over the crossroads signposted Mattingley to meet the B3349. Turn left signposted Reading and in about 1/2 mile leave the main road. Take the first turning on the right **E** signposted Mattingley Church to run through woods to a T-junction in Mattingley village. Turn right signposted Hazeley and then right again to the church car park. From here you can enjoy this peaceful corner of England of long ago – just a cluster of deep-eaved cottages around a wide green.

Retrace the route to the end of the lane which led to the church car park and turn right. After 1/2 mile turn right signposted Hazeley Bottom. In 1/2 mile turn right again signposted Dipley and West Green to run to a T-junction. Turn left to meet the A30 in Hartley Wintney. Turn right to drive through Phoenix Green back to Hook. ∎

The Church of St Mary the Virgin, Silchester, encircled by Roman walls

LYNDHURST, THE NORTH OF THE NEW FOREST AND THE AVON VALLEY

47 MILES – 4 HOURS
START AND FINISH AT LYNDHURST

This tour runs north from Lyndhurst and then follows the western boundary of the New Forest to give magnificent views over the Avon valley. On the way try to solve a mystery that has baffled historians for over eight hundred years – the untimely death of William Rufus in a Forest glen. The route leaves the Forest to cross the Avon valley and visit historic Breamore House and the nearby Saxon church. Peaceful lanes lead back to Lyndhurst past Bolderwood where wild fallow bucks graze in the meadows.

Bear in mind that Lyndhurst can become very busy during the summer.

Leave Lyndhurst on the A35 signposted Bournemouth. After ¼ mile, at Swan Green, turn right for Emery Down. The route takes you uphill between a row of picturesque thatched cottages and the village

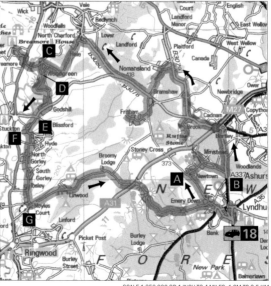

SCALE 1:250 000 OR 1 INCH TO 4 MILES *1 CM TO 2.5 KM*

cricket ground. **The road bears left through Emery Down.** Christ Church, on the left, was built of warm red brick in 1864 and was the gift of Admiral Boultbee. He also endowed the almshouses to the right of the

road known as 'Boultbee's cottages'. **Shortly after passing the almshouses you will see the New Forest Inn on your left. Ignore a joining road on the left just past the inn and continue along the right-hand road. After a mile pass the sign to Leominsted Fish Farm and the first road on the right. Turn right down the second road A.** There is no sign, but it is opposite a lane to a farm marked with a no-through-road symbol. Keep straight on downhill past all joining roads. Cross the ford in Newtown to run up to a T-junction. Turn right, signposted Cadnam, to the centre of Minstead. Just past the Trusty Servant Inn there is a parking area on the left. If this is full, turn right up the lane to the church where there is room to park.

To continue the tour, return to the road by which you entered the village. With

A restored sixteenth-century cottage stands in Furzey Gardens

the Trusty Servant Inn on your left keep ahead, following the Stoney Cross sign, for about ¼ mile. Turn left signposted Furzey Gardens. The lane winds up to the gravel entrance to the gardens on the left and car park.

Retrace the route turning right for the Trusty Servant Inn. Keep straight on through the centre of Minstead village, passing the green on your right. Continue for about

1¼ miles to meet the A337. Turn left **B** and drive for 1¾ miles to the Cadnam roundabout. Turn left following the signs for the A31. In ¼ mile, at the next roundabout, bear right under the motorway to take the B3079 signed Bramshaw. After a mile drive through Brook village and turn left following the sign for the Rufus Stone. The lane winds

past the Sir Walter Tyrrell Inn to car parks on the left. Opposite the car park stands the Rufus Stone shaped like a small tower with three sides. According to tradition, the oak tree which deflected the fatal arrow from Sir Walter Tyrrell's bow grew on the spot where the stone now stands. The arrow pierced the breast of William II and he died instantly. Misty oak tree glades still surround the stone and it would come as no surprise to see ghostly huntsmen riding through these ancient woods!

With the stone on your left, keep straight on past Upper Canterton, over a watersplash, to rejoin the B3079 at Brook. Turn left to a junction. Still following the B3079 bear right for Bramshaw. Beware, pigs tend to wander on and off the road here. The highlight of their year is the October pannage season when they feast on acorns and beech-mast. After the end of the village you will pass Bramshaw Church,

---

• PLACES OF INTEREST •

Lyndhurst
Lyndhurst is the 'capital' and administrative centre of the New Forest. Its name means 'the wood of the lime trees'. Today there are fewer limes, but the village is still surrounded by some of the finest oak and beech woods in the Forest.

A royal manor has stood at the top of the High Street since Saxon times and now a Queen Anne building stands on the same site, known as the Queen's House. Under the same roof is the ancient Verderers' Court dating from the fourteenth century. Originally established to administer the harsh Forest laws, the court meets today to settle a variety of claims and disputes.

The Victorian Church of St Michael and All Angels has a magnificent reredos by Lord Leighton and a splendid east window designed by the Pre-

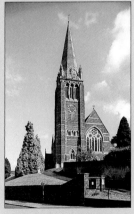

Raphaelite artists Morris, Burne-Jones and Kempe.

The New Forest Museum and Visitor Centre. A perfect introduction to this lovely area. It is adjacent to the large central car park. Open winter, daily, 10–5. Easter, 10–6. August 10–7.

Telephone: Southampton (01703) 283914

Minstead
This delightful Forest village is best explored on foot. The little church built of traditional Forest materials, wattle filled in with rubble and daub, has a charming cottage-like appearance. Inside there is a rare three-decker pulpit, a carved Saxon font, two galleries and interesting pews for the local gentlefolk – small rooms with comfortable seating, one even has a fireplace!

Furzey Gardens
A typical Forest garden with a pleasantly natural atmosphere. It is noted for its massed banks of azaleas, at their best in May and June. An old Forester's cottage stands in the grounds. Open daily, 10–5 (dusk in winter). Telephone: (01703) 812464

where traditionally Forest gypsies were married, on your right.

About a mile further on, just over a cattle-grid, turn left signposted Nomansland. The road runs beside green Forest lawns to Nomansland village. The village straggles along the Forest and, incidentally, the county boundary. The Lamb Inn is in Wiltshire, apart from the front step which is in Hampshire!

With the Lamb Inn on your right continue along the road beside Bramshaw Inclosure. The road bears left across heathland. Drive straight over the B3078. After about ½ mile turn right signposted Fritham and Eyeworth only. Follow the lane as it winds past scattered fields and farms. Commoners still exercise their ancient rights in Fritham, pasturing their cattle and ponies on the open Forest. **Eventually, you reach a large car park just past the Royal Oak pub. It is a good plan to leave your car here.** One of the Forest's loveliest surprises lies ahead, still concealed by trees. There is another car park further down the road, but this does get crowded in summer. So, if you can, walk the couple of hundred yards further down the road to see Eyeworth valley, a beautifully wooded glen sheltering a small lake. Footpaths lead through the woods beside the lake which is a haven for wildlife. The manager's house, which you will see to the left of the lane, is all that remains of the gunpowder works which once stood here. When returning to your car, look to the right of the lane when entering the car park to see the iron postbox which saved the postman from having to walk all the way to the manager's house.

Retrace the route from Fritham turning left at the T-junction and bearing left again shortly after at the Y-junction to rejoin the B3078. Turn left, signposted Fordingbridge and Downton, to a junction with the B3080.

The Rufus Stone in Canterton Glen in the New Forest

Bear right along the B3080 signposted Downton. After about 2 miles turn left along Tethering Drove for Hale and Woodgreen. Shortly you come to a crossroads. Turn left signposted Woodgreen Common. A beautiful road now runs beside the heath-covered valley of Hale Purlieu. A National Trust car park is on the left.

The road turns right to run downhill through Woodgreen village into the Avon valley. **At the T-junction in Woodgreen turn left and follow the main road round to the right, signposted Breamore. Cross the bridges over the River Avon and drive past the mill to meet the A338. Turn right along the A338 signed Salisbury and Downton and drive through Breamore village. Turn left following the signpost**

Rufus Stone, Canterton Glen
Historians still differ about the death of William Rufus which occurred on 1 August, 1100. Was it really an accident or was it murder? Did Walter Tyrrell really fire the fatal arrow? The King had many enemies including his own brothers – Robert, who was in Normandy at the time, and Henry, who immediately seized the Crown jewels and had himself crowned king. The Saxons, of course, hated him and many of his own nobles and churchmen had suffered from his cruelty. Walter Tyrrell denied firing the arrow even on his deathbed.

Breamore House and Countryside Museum
This Elizabethan house, built of warm red brick in 1583 by Queen Elizabeth's Treasurer, William Doddington, is set in beautiful parkland. It contains a fine collection of furniture, and the wood-panelled Great Hall, 85 feet (26 metres) in length, is hung with sixteenth- and seventeenth-century portraits. The former kitchen garden houses a countryside museum with village workshops and a reconstructed cottage. There is also a carriage museum featuring the 'Red Rover', the last stage coach to run between London and Southampton.

Teas and light lunches available. Open April–September, 2–5.30. Rest of year times vary. Telephone: (01725) 512233

Breamore Saxon Church
Among many outstanding features of this pre-Norman church is the carved Saxon rood over the south door and an Anglo-Saxon inscription over the arch in the south transept which reads 'Here is Manifested the Covenant to Thee'.

for Breamore House and Church. More signs direct you to the car park for Breamore House. Nearby is one of Hampshire's treasures, a magnificent Saxon church.

Retrace your route turning right through Breamore village and left over the River Avon towards Woodgreen. A few yards after entering Woodgreen turn right just past the village shop **C**. Continue uphill for about ¼ mile then be ready to turn right following the sign for Castle Hill **D**. The road now runs along the top of a ridge high above the Avon valley. There are car parks here and seats with splendid views of the river which winds like a silver ribbon through the watermeadows. Just before the road bends sharply left, the earth ramparts of an Iron Age fort crown Castle Hill on the right. To see the fort, stop in the second car park and walk beside the road, bearing a little right through the trees as you approach the left bend.

Drive round the bend to a T-junction. Turn right here to meet the B3078 at Godshill. Turn right signed Fording-bridge to descend into the valley. At the road junction turn right for a few yards then left signposted Stuckton **E**. The road bears right to a T-junction. Turn left through Stuckton. The road curves left and you need to look carefully for the right turn signposted North Gorley and Ringwood **F**. Turn right as the sign directs down Hyde Lane to a T-junction. Turn right, then, after a few yards, turn left for North Gorley. Follow the lane to this delectable village set around an open green where animals roam freely and ducks paddle happily round a reed and willow-fringed pond. Keep on along the lane signposted Ringwood and stay on the same lane (ignore the right turn for

Fordingbridge) as it curves left before continuing south along the western boundary of the Forest. Keep straight on for about a mile for Moyles Court. Just before the road dips to cross the ford over Dockens Water you will see Moyles Court on the right. This was the home of a Forest heroine, Dame Alice Lisle. Although her family supported King James, she nursed two wounded survivors of Monmouth's army after the battle of Sedgemoor. For this humanitarian deed she was beheaded in Winchester by order of Judge Jeffreys. After crossing the ford you reach a junction of several roads. Take the first road on the left **G**. A beautiful road now leads east over Forest heaths and wood-lands. There are frequent car parks and picnic spots. Ignore a joining road on the left and continue for Bolderwood and Emery Down to go under the A31. After ¼ mile look for a

wooden cross on the left flanked by two maple trees. This is a memorial to the Canadian soldiers who camped here on the eve of the D-Day landings. Just after the cross bear right along the gravelled track leading to Bolderwood car park. Waymarked Forest trails lead from here. To visit the deer hide, cross a lane at the far end of the car park and go through a small wooden gate leading down to the sanctuary.

Rejoin the road and turn right to follow the lane winding through oak and beech woods. After 2 miles you will see a parking area and picnic benches on the right. The large fireplace is a memorial to the Portuguese who helped with forestry work during the last war. Continue past two more car parks to a T-junction beside the New Forest Inn in Emery Down. Turn right to retrace your route to the A35 at Swan Green and turn left for Lyndhurst. ■

Breamore House, beautifully set in the Avon valley

THE SOLENT SHORE, BEAULIEU AND BUCKLERS HARD

65 MILES – 5 HOURS
START AND FINISH AT SOUTHAMPTON

This tour will interest all the family. The route follows quiet country lanes to Calshot, on the southern tip of Southampton Water, offering magnificent views of one of the world's greatest shipping lanes. It continues along the Solent shore to the famous gardens at Exbury, and then runs down to Beaulieu, in its picturesque riverside setting. Here, visits can be made to Lord Montagu's stately home Palace House, the abbey ruins and the National Motor Museum.

As these visits really require a full day it is a good plan to see this route as a 'menu', choose your favourites, and take several days to enjoy all the tour has to offer.

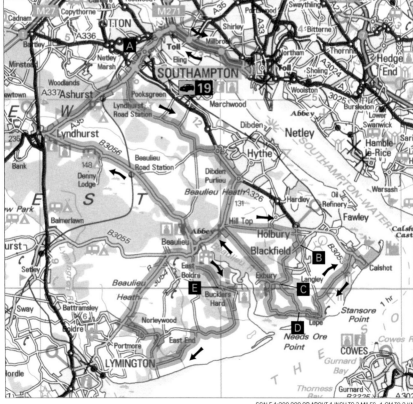

SCALE 1:200 000 OR ABOUT 1 INCH TO 3 MILES 1 CM TO 2 KM

This tour starts from Southampton Town Quay at the foot of the High Street. Follow the signs for The West, London and Winchester. At the roundabout keep heading west as indicated. Turn right at the traffic lights at the T-junction, signed Lyndhurst, and then left for Lyndhurst along the A3024 (A35). After about 3¹/₂ miles the road crosses the River Test at Redbridge. Keep ahead along the A35 signed Lyndhurst. Continue for about ¹/₂ mile to a roundabout .

From this point you may like to visit Eling Tide Mill. If so, turn left at the roundabout along the A326 signed Eling Tide Mill. Take the next road on the left, at the traffic lights (Jacobs Gutter Lane), signed Marchwood Military Port. Be ready to turn left again shortly after, signed Eling Tide Mill, to a T-junction. Bear left, signed Eling Mill, to pass the Church of St Mary the Virgin on the right . The road descends to a large car park on the left for the Tide Mill. Retrace the route from the car park, passing the church on the left and taking the first road on the right past the Village Bells pub. Continue by turning right at the T-junction, then right again along the A326 to rejoin the A35. Turn left to continue towards Lyndhurst.

If you do not wish to visit the mill keep straight on at the roundabout at . Keep ahead at the next roundabout. After about ¹/₂ mile turn left, signposted Longdown. This is Deerleap Lane, named after a leap of 18 yards (16 metres) once made by a deer in the nearby inclosure. The car park for Longdown Dairy Farm is about ¹/₄ mile further down the lane on the right. Continue down the lane to visit New Forest Nature Quest. The entrance is on the left.

Eling Tide Mill, possibly a unique survival of the use of tidal flow to operate machinery

As you continue along the lane meandering past small fields and farms, it is interesting to compare this cultivated landscape with the Forest heaths and woods over the meadows on the right. **After the road bears left to a T-junction, turn right. Shortly, the road** bends right – be careful as it is a sharp bend – to cross a cattle-grid and enter Forest heathland. At the crossroads turn left signposted Hythe and Fawley to drive up to a roundabout on the A326. Turn right for Fawley and continue along the A326

• PLACES OF INTEREST •

Eling Tide Mill
Eling is an oasis of green surrounding the estuary of Bartley Water. The mill is believed to be the only one in Western Europe still taking advantage of the tide to turn its wheels. Corn is ground to produce its own 'Canute' brand of flour. From the mill footpaths lead beside the stream and to the wharf colourful with small boats.

Mill open all year, Wednesday– Sunday, 10–4. Telephone: Southampton (01703) 869575

Longdown Dairy Farm
Children will enjoy a visit to this modern working farm where they can stroke and feed the friendly animals. Picnic and play areas, shop, refreshments.

Open 8 April–29 October, daily, 10–5. Telephone: (01703) 293326. For recorded information telephone: (01703) 293313

New Forest Nature Quest
A wide variety of wild creatures can be viewed in natural surroundings ranging from a typical back garden to the farmyard at night. Open daily, 10–5. Telephone: 01703 29216

Calshot
From 1913 Calshot served as a base for Naval sea planes which were flown to defend the Channel throughout the First World War. Between the wars Calshot hosted seaplanes designed by R. J. Mitchell who produced the Supermarine S6B which won the Schneider Trophy outright for Britain in 1931. Mitchell used the expertise he gained on seaplanes in his design for the Spitfire.

An exhibition in Calshot Castle tells the story of the former seaplane base. Open 1 April– 30 September, daily, 10–1 and 2–6. Telephone: (01703) 892023

Exbury Gardens
Two hundred acres of woodland gardens contain the Rothschild collection of azaleas and magnolias. Picnic areas, tearooms, shop and plant centre. Open 18 February–29 October, daily, 10–5.30 (or dusk if earlier). Telephone: (01703) 891203

Calsbot Castle walls still guard the approach to Southampton Water

to the next roundabout. **Turn right along the B3054, signposted Beaulieu, to cross Beaulieu Heath to the road junction at Hill Top. Turn left for Fawley.** The Dark Water is crossed at Ipers Bridge and the route now leaves the present boundaries of the Forest to visit the Solent shore.

Keep ahead for nearly a mile to the traffic lights. Turn right signposted Lepe. In just over ¼ mile look carefully for a sign on the left indicating the next turn which is right for Exbury **B**. You are surrounded, briefly, by Forest scenes as the road crosses Blackwell Common towards the line of trees fringing the Dark Water. **The road crosses the stream then climbs and turns left.** Darkwater car park, giving access to paths along the tree-covered hillsides bordering the Dark Water, is on the right.

Follow the road round a right bend to a T-junction **C**. **Turn left signposted Lepe to continue towards the coast. When you approach the shore turn left at the T-junction** **D** **signposted Langley and Blackfield.** The road follows the shoreline giving splendid views over the Solent to the Isle of Wight. **Continue to the large car park near Lepe beach and country park where you can picnic and enjoy sea views.**

The route turns north from the beach. After ½ mile take the first road on the right signposted Calshot. The road runs through a gentle countryside of small fields and copses and crosses the tangled marshes near Cadland House. **It then bears left to meet the B3053 at Ower. Turn right following the sign to the beach. When the road divides at the one-way system take the left-hand road. Park at Calshot beach or, alternatively, keep ahead following the road that runs along the narrow spit of land past Calshot Activities Centre to the car park close to Calshot Castle.** Henry VIII's small grey-walled castle still stands at the end of the spit, guarding the entrance to Southampton Water.

Retrace the route turning left in Ower for Lepe and then left at the T-junction for Lepe beach. Keep on to **D**. **Leave the former route here and bear left signposted Inchmery.** A beautiful road follows the coast to the entrance to the Beaulieu River and then turns right for Exbury. The entrance to Exbury Gardens is on the left.

Continue along Summer Lane to Hill Top. Turn left for a few yards, then left again down the B3054 for Beaulieu. The road drops to the riverside with the grey stone walls of the abbey precinct on the right. On the left, lawns reach down to the water – a perfect place to picnic

and feed the ducks. As the road curves left to cross the river, you will see Palace House, the home of Lord Montagu, among the trees on the right. It overlooks a wide stretch of water which was formerly the monks' fish pond. The house, abbey ruins and nearby National Motor Museum are open to the public – you will pass the entrance later in the tour.

Beaulieu village, its cottages built of russet-coloured bricks, is well worth exploring. **If you would like to stop in the village, keep to the B3054 as it crosses the foot of the High Street and continue for a few yards along the B3056.** The car park is on the left.

If you do not wish to stop, continue past the car park entrance to a T-junction and turn left, signposted Brockenhurst. Continue uphill for a short distance. Leave the B3054 and take the lane ahead signposted Bucklers Hard. After 2 miles drive straight ahead into Bucklers Hard car park. Some of the great warships for Nelson's fleet were built of sturdy Forest oak here. A double row of cottages set behind wide lawns runs down to the old slipways on the Beaulieu River. Linger here to visit the excellent museum and restored cottages, walk beside the river or take a boat trip.

From the car park retrace the route, past a lane on the left . Take the second lane on the left **E** **signposted St Leonards and Sowley.** The road runs south for about a mile and then turns sharply right past the ruins of St Leonard's Chapel and Grange. **Pass a turning on the right and keep ahead for Sowley. Turn left down Sowley Lane.** Pass Sowley Pond, once the monks' fish pond. In the seventeenth and eighteenth centuries there was an ironworks here with water-powered tilt-hammers working ironstone brought from Hengistbury Head and the beaches at Hordle.

Beaulieu

Saxon *beo-ley*, the bee meadow, became French *beau lieu*, beautiful place, when interpreted by the Norman scribes compiling the Domesday Book. There could be no better description of this lovely riverside village overlooked by Palace House and the ruins of its Cistercian abbey. According to the Saxon chroniclers this huge estate of 10,000 acres was granted, reluctantly, by King John to twelve Cistercian monks in 1204, with unique rights to the bed of the Beaulieu River. Thriving on their wool and tariffs charged on waterborne trade the monks built a splendid monastery with a huge church, the outlines of which can still be traced. Here, they cared for the sick, educated children, sheltered travellers and offered the right of sanctuary to fugitives.

After the Dissolution much of the stone was carted away to build coastal defences, but the ruined cloisters are still beautiful, and some buildings remain, including the monks' refectory which is now the parish church.

At the Dissolution the land was bought by Thomas Wriothesley, an ancestor of Lord Montagu, who owns the estate today. The fourteenth-century gatehouse has become his home, Palace House.

In the grounds is the **National Motor Museum**, a priceless collection of 250 classic, vintage and veteran motor cars. Picnic areas, cafeterias and bars. Open daily, 10–5pm. Easter–September, 10–6. Telephone: Beaulieu (01590) 612123 or 612345

Bucklers Hard

A visit to this unspoilt eighteenth-century village is a 'must' for all visitors to the New Forest. You can share the day-to-day life of the shipbuilders of the time in their cottages and see them relaxing over a mug of ale in the local inn. The museum tells the fascinating story of the village and contains an

exhibition devoted to Sir Francis Chichester who began his voyage round the world in *Gypsy Moth IV* from Bucklers Hard.

The museum is open September–March, daily, 10–4.30. Easter–May, 10–6. May–September, 10–9. Telephone: (01590) 616203

Beaulieu Road Station

Pony sales are held here six times a year from August to December and also in April. For times see local papers or contact the Beaulieu Road pub (01703) 292342.

The road curves right sign-posted for Boldre, Lymington and Beaulieu. Continue past a joining road on the left for East End and Boldre. Cross the bridge in East End. At the Y-junction turn left signposted Norleywood and Boldre. The road turns right to run through Norleywood village and past Norley Inclosure to meet the B3054. Turn right along the B3054 which crosses the southern part of Beaulieu Heath. Hatchet Pond on the left – formerly a marl pit – is now a haven for wildlife. There is a car park by the pond.

Past the pond, bear right for Beaulieu keeping to the B3054. This road joins the B3056 which runs left to by-pass Beaulieu village. Follow the signs for Lyndhurst. Now you have a splendid view over the water to Palace House. The entrance to the Beaulieu complex is clearly signed off the B3056 on the right.

To continue the tour follow the B3056, still following the signs for Lyndhurst. The road crosses the railway at Beaulieu Road Station. After crossing the heath, the road runs close to two of the finest 'ancient and ornamental' woods in the Forest, Denny and Matley. Here you will find the massive oaks, their branches draped with ivy and ferns, for which the Forest is famous. A car park on the right at the approach to Matley also provides access to Denny. The road meets the A35 just east of Lyndhurst. If you wish to visit the village, turn left and then left again to the car park entrance on the right.

If not, turn right along the A35 which leads to the A3024 and follow the signs back to Southampton. Turn right following the signs for the Old Town and Waterfront to return to Town Quay.

Palace House, Beaulieu, once the gatehouse of a Cistercian monastery

LYMINGTON, BROCKENHURST AND THE SOUTHERN NEW FOREST

49 MILES – 4 HOURS
START AND FINISH AT LYMINGTON

Some of the most beautiful areas of the New Forest can be enjoyed on this tour including the Ornamental Drive, the old smuggling village of Burley overlooked by its Iron Age hill-fort, and High Corner in the remote valley of Dockens Water. You will see the oldest church at Brockenhurst, the oldest oak at Knightwood, and the oldest inn at Pilley. You will also see the home and grave of a New Forest heroine, Alice Lisle, whose statue stands in the Commons' corridor in the Houses of Parliament.

Leave Lymington heading north on the A337, signed Lyndhurst and Brockenhurst. About ³/₄ mile from the town centre, just after the B3054 leads right from a roundabout, you will see the earth ramparts of the Forest's largest Iron Age hill-fort, Buckland Rings, on the left of the road. **Follow the A337 under the railway and continue for another 3 miles to approach the railway at the level-crossing in Brockenhurst. Before the crossing turn right for a few yards up the lane signposted St Nicholas Parish Church** ▲. It is the oldest church in the Forest and is mentioned in the Domesday Book.

Retrace your route and turn right over the crossing.

Just past the crossing turn left into Brockenhurst village. Keep ahead for the village centre, cross the B3055 and continue down the High Street. Drive over the watersplash at the end of the street to a T-junction. Turn right along Rhinefield road. The road curves left to run over spacious heaths towards the woods fringing Ober Water. There are several car parks and picnic places. The best is at Puttles Bridge. There are two parks with this sign – the more attractive one is on the right as the road bears right to enter the woods. A way-marked Forest trail leads from the car park beside Ober Water.

Now you are reaching the most beautiful part of the Ornamental Drive – a narrow road linking Brockenhurst with the A35 and the A31. Originally it was a gravel track serving as a coaching route providing access to the old Forest Manor of Bolderwood and Rhinefield House. About ¹/₄ mile past Puttles Bridge, look left for a fine view of Rhinefield House, a Gothic-style mansion built by Lieutenant Munro Walker in 1887. The Ornamental Drive bears right to the Blackwater car park on the right. This section is planted with exotic trees, including wellingtonias (the tallest trees in the Forest) and redwoods. From here you can follow three waymarked trails.

To continue the tour follow the Ornamental Drive past Brock Hill car park on the left (also providing access to the trails) to meet the A35. Drive straight across the A35 to continue along

Rhinefield House is mock-Gothic in style

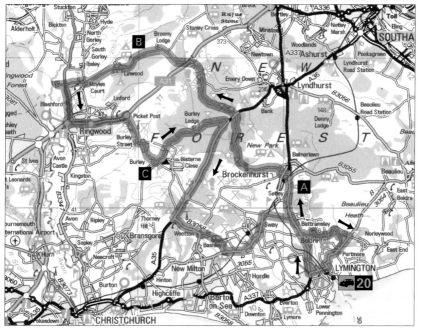

the Ornamental Drive. After a few yards turn right into the first car park on the right at Knightwood. Among other mighty pollarded trees stands the oldest oak in the Forest, reputed to have stood in this sunny glade for up to 600 years. It is 100 feet (31 metres) tall and has a girth of 23 feet (7 metres). This kingly tree stands in the centre of the aptly-named 'Monarch's Grove'. To mark the ninth centenary of the Forest in 1970, the Queen planted an oak a short distance away. A twenty-minute circular trail, suitable for prams and push-chairs, leads round the grove.

Follow the Ornamental Drive for about another mile. Look left now as you pass the magnificent beech woods at Mark Ash, the finest in the Forest. **About ¼ mile further on cross a cattle-grid and turn immediately right into Bolderwood car park.** More waymarked trails lead from here. Walk through the small wooden gate (it is on the left as you turn into the car park) to visit the hide which overlooks the Bolderwood Deer Sanctuary. Herds of wild

• PLACES OF INTEREST •

Lymington
This old port is situated at the lowest fording point of the Lymington River as it flows between marshes into the Solent. Until the middle of the eighteenth century, when the Toll Bridge Dam was built across the river, Lymington flourished as a port noted for its trade in salt from the pans fringing the Solent shore and for its smuggling activities.

The town is a charming mix of elegant Georgian houses and neat bow-fronted cottages often grouped around small courts and alleyways bright with flowers. A picturesque cobbled street winds down to the quayside. There is a commercial fishing fleet, two large marinas and river moorings attracting yachts from all parts of the world.

A regular ferry service runs from Lymington to Yarmouth on the Isle of Wight. Telephone: Lymington (01590) 673301

Free guided walks around Lymington are organised in the summer. Telephone: (01590) 644438 or 679391

Brockenhurst
Once you leave the busy High Street, Brockenhurst becomes a true Forest village, rambling around small heaths and woods, giving unexpected glimpses of attractive cottages facing lawns cropped short by wild ponies.

The church dates from the twelfth century, although Saxon masonry can be seen in its walls. The arch over the south doorway is beautifully carved. Inside is a curtained 'Squire's pew'. On the east side of the churchyard you will find the beautifully kept memorial to the New Zealand and Indian soldiers who lie there. During the First World War Brockenhurst was the home of a base hospital. You will also find the grave of a celebrated local snake-catcher, 'Brusher' Mills. He lived in a simple hut in the Forest and used to entertain travellers taking the coach to Bournemouth from Brockenhurst station with the snakes he kept in his pockets.

91

The Knightwood Oak is the oldest oak tree in the New Forest

fallow deer can usually be seen in the meadows.

Drive down the gravel track from the car park to a road. Turn left and, after about ¼ mile, you will see the Canada Cross, flanked by two maple trees, on the right overlooking the valley of Highland Water. This is a memorial to the Canadian soldiers who camped here on the eve of D-Day. **Follow the road as it runs under the A31 and through the pines of Slufters Inclosure to Broomy Heath. After passing a joining road on the right, the route bears left signposted Linwood and Ringwood.**

A mile further on a diversion can be made to see a beautiful part of the Dockens Water valley. Turn right down a rather bumpy track signposted High Corner Inn 🄱. You can park in the valley and walk down to the stream – an ideal place for a picnic.

Retrace your route to the road and turn right to continue through the Forest for about 2½ miles to a crossroads on the Forest's western boundary. Turn right signposted Mockbeggar and N. Gorley, to cross the ford over Dockens Water, and

then, **almost immediately, left signposted Ringwood and Ellingham.**

On the right is Moyles Court. In the seventeenth century it was the home of a brave lady, Alice Lisle. She is buried in Ellingham churchyard. **To see her grave, turn right at the T-junction just past the house. The road bears left to cross the Avon valley. Drive straight over the A338, signposted Ellingham Church, past the no-through-road sign. After a few yards the road bears right for Ellingham Church where there is a large car park.** Alice Lisle is buried in a table tomb to the right of the porch under the window.

Retrace the route to the A338 and turn right signed Ringwood to drive south down the Avon valley. At the roundabout bear left to join the A31 signed Stoney Cross

and Cadnam. **After 2 miles pull off left at Picket Post signed Burley. The road turns right under the A31 in the direction of Burley.** The ridge ahead, Castle Hill, is crowned by the earth ramparts of an Iron Age hill-fort. **The road rises to a T-junction and then bears left. Pass a joining road on the left to drive through Burley Street and then Burley village, towards the war memorial at the top of the High Street. Turn left past the Queen's Head pub. Do not follow the main road uphill, but continue straight on down the lane ahead signposted Burley Church 🄲.** Once Burley was a remote Forest village relying for its income on its yearly crop of acorns and beech-mast, now it is a busy tourist centre. But it still retains a great deal of its charm. Forest trees shade its many tiny lanes

The Canada Cross overlooking the pine-clad slopes of Highland Water

• PLACES OF INTEREST •

Moyles Court and Alice Lisle, near Ringwood
After the defeat of the Duke of Monmouth's army at Sedgemoor, two wounded survivors, Hicks and Nelthorpe, made their way to the Forest and were found exhausted by Alice Lisle in the grounds of her home, Moyles Court. Although she was a staunch Royalist and her husband was fighting for the King, she sheltered and nursed the wounded men. For this humane act the notorious Judge Jeffreys ordered her to be beheaded. The gallant old lady died maintaining she was no traitor.

Burley
Burley means 'a fortified place', and the first settlement in the area must have been the Iron Age fort crowning the high moorland ridge to the west of the village. Below the fort a Saxon war path runs to Ringwood in the Avon valley, the route possibly followed

by the Saxon invaders who, in AD 519, defeated the Britons close to the Avon at 'Cerdices ford', today's Charford.

A stranger battle took place on nearby Burley Beacon. Here, according to a document in Berkeley Castle, the redoubtable Sir Moris Berkeley overcame 'a devouring dragon'!

Boldre Church
Boldre church is known nationally as 'The Hood' church. HMS *Hood*, sunk in action against the *Bismark* in 1941, had been the flagship of Vice-Admiral L. E. Holland who died in the action. He had been a regular worshipper at Boldre, and his widow arranged for an illuminated book of remembrance containing the names of all who died to be placed in the church. A commemoration service is held yearly on the Sunday nearest to 24 May, the date of the sinking.

are set among the meadows bordering the Lymington River. **Cross the bridge and keep to the same road as it bears right.** Shortly a road on the right is signposted Spinners Gardens which you might like to visit.

To continue the tour, keep ahead through Pilley past the school. On the right you will see the oldest inn in the Forest, the Fleur de Lys, long and low with whitewashed half-timbered walls under a deep-thatched roof. It is reputed to date from the eleventh century.

If you would like to see Boldre Church, famous for its associations with HMS *Hood* and William Gilpin, the author of books on the 'picturesque', take the next road on the left after the inn (Church Lane) which runs up to Boldre Church where there is a car park. Then retrace your route turning left at the end of Church Lane.

Keep straight on ignoring all side roads past the pond in Pilley Bailey. The road bends right, and then left at Bull Hill to bring you to the B3054. Turn right signposted Lymington and follow the signs for the town to cross the bridge over the river. Drive over the level crossing and, if you follow the road left at the T-junction, it will bring you to the foot of Lymington High Street. ∎

and donkeys look in at the Post Office windows. **Follow the lane past Burley Manor, now a hotel, on your left to meet the A35. Turn right along the A35, signed Bournemouth and Christchurch, and continue for 4 miles. Turn left signposted Wootton along the B3058. As you approach the Rising Sun Inn at Wootton, follow the road ahead signed Lymington, Sway (B3055) and Tiptoe. So, on the corner, leave the B3058 and turn left for only a few yards to a Y-junction. Take the right-hand road signposted Sway and Lymington. Follow this road for about a mile to meet the B3055. Turn left signposted Sway and Brockenhurst.** The road runs through Arnewood, a pleasantly leafy district, made famous as 'Arnwood', the home of the Beverley family in *The Children of the New Forest*. Captain Marryat wrote the book while staying at the Chewton Glen, now a hotel.

Keep straight on over all crossroads to drive through Durns Town, the oldest part of Sway village. Pass a joining road on the left and, a few yards further on, turn right, signposted Boldre and Lymington. At the A337 turn right. After ³/₄ mile turn left signposted Boldre. The road runs down into this charming village where old Forest cottages and elegant Georgian houses

Cobbled Quay Street in Lymington leads down to the river

USEFUL ADDRESSES AND INFORMATION

For information on daily events and weather forecasts:
BBC Dorset 103.8MHz
BBC Radio Solent 300/211m; 999/1359KHz; 96.1MHz
Two Counties Radio 362m; 828KHz; 102.3MHz

Hampshire County Council Information Centres

Winchester
Mottisfont Court,
High Street, Hampshire
Tel: Winchester (01962) 870500

Portsmouth
Central Library, Hampshire
Tel: (01345) 626100

Basingstoke
The Library, Hampshire
Tel: (01345) 626424

National Trust Regional Offices

Dorset
Eastleigh Court, Bishopstrow,
Warminster,Wiltshire BA12 9HW
Tel: Warminster (01985) 843600

Hampshire
The Southern Regional Office,
Polesden Lacey, Dorking,
Surrey RH5 6BD
Tel: Dorking (01372) 453401

Tourist Boards

Hampshire and Eastern Dorset
Southern Tourist Board
40 Chamberlayne Road,
Eastleigh, Hampshire SO5 5JH
Tel: Southampton (01703) 620006

West Dorset
West Country Tourist Board
60 St David's Hill, Exeter,
Devon EX4 4SY
Tel: Exeter (01392) 420891

Tourist Information Centres

Opening times vary – check by telephone

Dorset

Blandford Forum
Marsh and Ham Car Park,
West Street, Dorset DT11 7AW
Tel: Blandford Forum (01258) 454770

Bournemouth
Westover Road, Dorset BH1 2BU
Tel: Bournemouth (01202) 294808

Bridport
32 South Street, Dorset DT6 3NQ
Tel: Bridport (01308) 424901

Christchurch
23 High Street, Dorset BH23 1AB
Tel: Christchurch (01202) 471780

Dorchester
Unit 11, Antelope Walk,
Dorset DT1 1BE
Tel: Dorchester (01305) 267992

Lyme Regis
Guildhall Cottage, Church Street,
Dorset DT7 3BS
Tel: Lyme Regis (01297) 442138

Poole
The Quay, Dorset BH15 1HE
Tel: Poole (01202) 673322

Shaftesbury
8 Bell Street, Dorset SP7 8AE
Tel: Shaftesbury (01747) 853514

Sherborne
3 Tilton Court, Digby Road,
Dorset DT9 3NL
Tel: Sherborne (01935) 815341

Swanage
The White House, Shore Road,
Dorset BH19 1LB
Tel: Swanage (01929) 422885

Wareham
Town Hall, East Street,
Dorset BH20 4NG
Tel: Wareham (01929) 552740

Weymouth
The King's Statue, The Esplanade,
Dorset DT4 7AN
Tel: Weymouth (01305) 765221 or 765223

Wimborne Minster
29 High Street, Dorset BH21 1HR
Tel: Wimborne Minster (01202) 886116

Hampshire

Aldershot
Military Museum, Queen's Avenue,
Hampshire GU11 2LG
Tel: Aldershot (01252) 20968

Alton
7 Cross and Pillory Lane,
Hampshire GU34 1HL
Tel: Alton (01420) 88448

Andover
Town Mill House, Bridge Street,
Hampshire SP10 1BL
Tel: Andover (01264) 324320

Basingstoke
Willis Museum, Old Town Hall,
Market Place, Hampshire RG21 1QD
Tel: Basingstoke (01256) 817618

Eastleigh
Town Hall Centre, Leigh Road,
Hampshire SO50 4DE
Tel: Southampton (01703) 641261

Fareham
Westbury Manor, West Street,
Hampshire PO16 0JJ
Tel: Fareham (01329) 221342 or 824896

Fleet
The Harlington Centre, Fleet Road,
Hampshire GU13 8BY
Tel: Fleet (01252) 811151

Fordingbridge
Salisbury Street, Hampshire SP6 1AB
Tel: Fordingbridge (01425) 654560

Gosport
Gosport Museum, Walpole Road,
Hampshire PO12 1NS
Tel: Gosport (01705) 522944

Havant
1 Park Road South,
Hampshire PO9 1HA
Tel: Havant (01705) 480024

Lymington
St. Barb Museum and Visitor Centre
New Street, Hampshire
Tel: Lymington (01590) 672422

Lyndhurst and New Forest
New Forest Museum and Visitor Centre
Main Car Park, Hampshire SO43 7NY
Tel: Southampton (01703) 284404

Petersfield
County Library, 27 The Square,
Hampshire GU32 3HH
Tel: Petersfield (01730) 268829

Portsmouth
The Hard, Hampshire PO1 3QJ
Tel: Portsmouth (01705) 826722

102 Commercial Road,
Hampshire PO1 1EJ
Tel: Portsmouth (01705) 838382

Clarence Esplanade
Southsea, Hampshire PO5 3ST
Tel: Portsmouth (01705) 832464

Ringwood
The Furlong, Hampshire BH24 1AZ
Tel: Ringwood (01425) 470896

Romsey
1 Latimer Street, Hampshire SO51 8DF
Tel: Romsey (01794) 512987

Southampton
Above Bar, Hampshire SO9 4XF
Tel: Southampton (01703) 221106

Winchester
Guildhall, The Broadway,
Hampshire SO23 9LJ
Tel: Winchester (01962) 840500 or 848180

Other Useful Organisations

The Council for the Protection of Rural England
25 Buckingham Palace Road,
London SE1W OPP
Tel: (0171) 9766433

The Countryside Commission
John Dower House,
Crescent Place, Cheltenham,
Gloucestershire GL50 3RA
Tel: Cheltenham (01242) 521381

English Heritage
Keysign House, 429 Oxford Street,
London W1R 2HD
Tel: (0171) 973 3000 (Enquiries)

The Forestry Commission
Information Branch,
231 Corstorphine Road,
Edinburgh EH12 7AT
Tel: Edinburgh (0131) 334 0303

National Trust
36 Queen Anne's Gate,
London SW1H 9AS
Tel: (0171) 227 4810

Ordnance Survey
Romsey Road, Maybush,
Southampton SO16 4GU
Tel: 0345 330011 (Lo-call)

INDEX